RESET
— FOR —
PARENTS

HOW TO KEEP YOUR KIDS FROM BACKSLIDING

TODD FRIEL

What Others Are Saying about Reset for Parents . . .

Hard hitting. Theologically sound. Desperately needed.
> — Ray Comfort, Living Waters

If more parents understood their biblical responsibility in the discipleship of their children, there would be less 1 John 2:19 teens roaming around on the university campuses. Todd Friel is not just a good radio and television show host, he knows the Bible and is a good communicator of biblical truth. This book is a helpful resource for the church today.
> — Dr. Josh Buice, Pray's Mill Baptist Church

Todd is "at it" again. Thankfully, that is a good thing. Why? Because Friel's weapon of choice is not his own wit or wisdom (which he has gobs of), but rather, it is the Word of God. In *Reset for Parents* you will be able to "hear" his voice, one desperately wanting its readers to believe the good news about parenting. If you want minimalistic moralism, go elsewhere. If you want a book laced with the tincture of the Gospel, grab a comfy chair and be prepared to be graciously tilted.
> — Mike Abendroth, Pastor of Bethlehem Bible Church and
>   host of No Compromise Radio You

Reset for Parents is far more than just a solid, biblical resource — it's a counselor, an encourager, and a wise mentor that deals with the heart of the problem — which is the problem of the heart. This book is a magnum opus on gardening. But it won't teach you how to whack weeds at ground level; it will show you how to go for the root. It will instruct you in how to till the soil of your children's hearts in such a way that they will be primed to receive the seed of God's Word — bringing about an abundant harvest of eternal fruit for the glory of God. Its principles are a must-learn, a must-do, and a must-share.
> — Emeal Zwayne, President, Living Waters

Too many evangelical books on parenting focus entirely on the work of training our kids to *behave*. While that's an important aspect of every parent's duty, Christian moms and dads have an even higher calling: teaching our children to *believe* — modeling the faith for them, faithfully living by the truth of God's Word, raising our kids in the nurture and admonition of the Lord, and thereby pointing them to Christ. Todd Friel brilliantly summarizes the essential whys and hows of gospel-centered parenting.
> — Phil Johnson, Executive Director, Grace to You

This book will bring you to your knees and lift you up to serve your children with more intentionality and more humility.
> — Tedd Tripp, President, Shepherding the Heart Ministries

"Target your parenting toward salvation, not behavior." If you are a parent, that single sentence tells you why this book is not optional. I've never seen a parenting book so rich in theology, church history, and tactics for engaging our kids not only in their daily hiccups, but on the foundational questions of life. I'm not surprised. Todd's book is well-written because his life is well-lived. I know this to be true. I've worked with Todd in the studio. I've seen him in times of great joy and under tough deadlines behave as a gospel-driven soldier for Christ. I trust him to speak candidly into my life, to challenge me, knowing I will be a better man for it. And you can trust him to speak to your parenting through a crystal-clear biblical lens.

— Scott Klusendorf, President, Life Training Institute

"Training youth in the truth" is more than just a slogan today. It's more important than ever that we equip our children and teens with biblical truths: we must counteract the huge exodus of young people from our churches. Our research has shown that even in middle school, many of our teens are beginning to doubt the accuracy of God's Word. And in many of their minds, they are already checking out of church. I praise God that Todd has a passion to help parents and church leaders rescue their youth and have them walk in truth, especially the truth of the gospel. Parents will find Todd's book to be a powerful Bible-based how-to guide in improving their parenting skills.

— Ken Ham, co-author of the book *Already Gone*, on why
teens and young adults are leaving the church

I love *Reset for Parents* and wish it was written 25 years ago. Authored by a seasoned parent, this thoughtfully written and well-paced book comes with loads of specifics and practical examples. But at its core is a transcendent gospel paradigm, rooted in Law and grace, that can be applied in all situations for the benefit of parents and children alike. If you want to raise self-righteous Pharisees, this isn't the book for you. But if you want to raise good repenters who believe the gospel and cherish it deeply, then you will find much help for yourself on these pages.

— Milton Vincent, author, *The Gospel Primer*

This new book, *Reset for Parents*, is a much-needed antidote for the plague that is crippling the Church today, namely the tragedy of children raised in Christian homes, but who abandon the faith when they go away to college. Every parent needs to take this message to heart and implement its truths in their childrearing. I have been privileged to be in the Friel household and have seen firsthand the positive results of this biblical teaching at work. This is a man who practices what he preaches.

— Dr. Steve Lawson
Founder and CEO of One Passion Ministries

First printing: February 2017

Copyright © 2017 by Todd Friel. All rights reserved. No part of this book may be used or reproduced in any manner whatsoever without written permission from the publisher, except in the case of brief quotations in articles and reviews. For information write:

New Leaf Press, P.O. Box 726, Green Forest, AR 72638
New Leaf Press is a division of the New Leaf Publishing Group, Inc.

ISBN: 978-0-89221-752-6
Library of Congress Number: 2016920255

Cover by Felicia Joyce Designs, LLC
Photo credit page 191: Emily Friel

Please consider requesting that a copy of this volume be purchased by your local library system.

Printed in the United States of America

Please visit our website for other great titles:
www.newleafpress.net

For information regarding author interviews,
please contact the publicity department at (870) 438-5288.

New Leaf Press
A Division of New Leaf Publishing Group
www.newleafpress.net

Dedication

To my beloved children, Emily, Haley, and Jack. I am over the moon excited that my children are walking in the truth (3 John 4). I love you profoundly and I only wish I were half the parent this book describes. I am a million times sorry for all of the times I have failed you. I beg your forgiveness. May you do a thousand times better than your dad did.

To my wife, who knows I am not the man this book describes, thank you for being patient with me. I love you more every day.

To Dr. Tedd Tripp, your fingerprints are all over chapter 3. Thank you.

To Rick Thomas, 1 Corinthians 6:1–8 forbids lawsuits against fellow believers. Keep that in mind as you read my plagiarism of your excellent work in chapter 2.

Contents

Why Parents Need a Reset

Before you know it, your son or daughter will be moving out, possibly to attend a university or tech school. Would you like to hear how your child is likely to sound after being out of the nest for three months?

> *Me:* Hello young person.
> *Your child:* Hello, Sir.
> *Me:* Are you a born-again Christian?
> *Your child:* Yes, I am.
> *Me:* If someone is not a born-again Christian like you, will that person go to hell?
> *Your child:* I don't want to judge.
> *Me:* Sigh.

I have had that conversation hundreds, possibly thousands, of times. I have also had this dialogue with countless "Christian" students:

> *Me:* Hello young person.
> *Your child:* Hello, Sir.
> *Me:* Are you a born-again Christian?
> *Your child:* I used to be, but I'm kind of re-thinking all that stuff.
> *Me:* Deep sigh.

And finally, there is this heartbreaker:

> *Me:* Hello young person.
> *Your child:* Hello, Sir.
> *Me:* Are you a born-again Christian?

9

Your child: I'd rather not talk about it.

Me: Why not?

Your child: If my parents find out what I have been doing here, they wouldn't be happy.

Me: Very deep sigh.

All three of these conversations reveal that these kids really don't understand biblical Christianity, even though they were raised in a Christian home like yours. The odds that your child won't apostatize and talk exactly like those "backslidden" kids are not in your favor.

Pick your favorite pollster and you will be horrified to discover that the MAJORITY of our Christian youth will spend their formative years at church playing gross-out games, only to leave home and notoriously "lose their faith." Today's headlines makes this crystal clear.

> *Headline:* Young Christians Highly Involved in Porn (one-newsnow.com)
>
> *Headline:* Christian Teens Are Viewing More Porn Than Ever Before (patheos.com)
>
> *Headline:* Most American Teens Hold Positive Opinion of Bible but Rarely Read It, Survey Finds (Christianpost.com)
>
> *Headline:* Why Young Christians Can't Grasp Our Arguments against Gay "Marriage" (Lifesitenews.com)
>
> *Headline:* For Millennials, Out-of-Wedlock Childbirth Is the Norm (Slate.com)

On and on the headlines go, all pointing in the same direction: we are losing an entire generation of Christian youth. The statistics that state 60 to 80 percent of our kids "lose the faith" reveals that Christian parents are producing more false converts than true.

Clearly, we are doing something radically wrong. It is time for an examination of our Christian parenting methods and ask, "Do I need a parenting reset?"

The Goal

Reset for Parents is NOT about:

> ➤ Teaching your children manners.

➤ Changing your children's behavior.
➤ Getting your unruly children under control.

Instead, *Reset for Parents* is written to help you lovingly and relentlessly pursue the one thing every parent wants more than anything else: to see his or her children walking in the truth.

Reset for Parents is written for you to consider your parenting priorities, and possibly reorient and aim toward one overarching goal: *the salvation of your children.*

➤ *Reset for Parents* is not a parenting manual; it is a salvation guide.
➤ *Reset for Parents* will not help you change your child's diaper; but it will help you apply your faith to the heart of your child.
➤ *Reset for Parents* aims to encourage you to stop raising well-behaved children and start raising children who love Jesus . . . who will then desire to be well-behaved.
➤ *Reset for Parents* is not about changing your children; it is about changing YOU.

What you are about to read is not the musings of a Christian father who raised his kids perfectly. Instead, you are going to read about the consistent excuses I have amassed after witnessing to hundreds (perhaps thousands) of university students who "backslid."

You can avoid those mistakes. You do not have to become a member of the prodigal children club. However, you are likely going to have to reset your parenting approach and raise your children in a radically different fashion than you currently are.

Let me applaud you for making the effort to accomplish the most important assignment a Christian parent has — to raise up your children in the discipline and instruction of the Lord (Ephesians 6: 4).

Reset for Parents cannot guarantee that your child will get saved. But it does promise that if you apply what you are about to read, you may hear the sweetest words that anyone can hear, "Well done, my good and faithful servant [Matthew 25:21], your children will be here soon."

Are you ready for a reset?

Chapter 1

Stop Disciplining and Start Discipling

Dear Mom and Dad, if you want the joy of watching your child grow in love for the Lord and obedience to you (Proverbs 29:17), I beg you to thoughtfully consider this advice:

> Every interaction with your child should have one overarching goal: that your words and actions would lead them to love and fear the Lord more than they currently do.

In other words, stop striving for peace, quiet, and well-behaved children. Start focusing primarily on your child's salvation. That one thought will forever change you, your child, and your home. If your family is like ours, this will likely require considerable adjustments in your parenting strategy. So, let me phrase this negatively:

> If your interaction with your child doesn't end with more love, joy and peace than when you began, then you have failed in your one and only assignment with your child.

The salvation of your child is eternally more important than compliance.

> ➤ Who cares if your child holds his fork right, but dies and goes to hell?
> ➤ Who cares if your child never uses a potty word, but spends eternity crying out for a drop of water?
> ➤ Who cares if your child gets accepted by an Ivy League school, but experiences the wrath of God forever and ever?

Because the salvation of our children is the most urgent issue for our children, doesn't it make sense that you and I focus tenaciously on that objective? What does it profit a parent if their child never gets arrested, but languishes in an eternal prison?

God wants your children to love Him. God wants your children to run to Him. God wants your children to find their hope, joy, and peace in Him. If you and I are not working with God to that end, then we are working against Him. Let's begin the reset.

Disciplining Vs. Discipling

This may be the most radical Christian parenting advice you will ever hear: NEVER discipline your child; instead, ALWAYS disciple your child. Let me 'splain myself, Lucy.

What I am not saying:

> ➤ I am not saying you should never spank your child.
> ➤ I am not saying you should never give your child orders.
> ➤ I am not saying you should never correct your child's behavior.

What I am saying:

> ➤ If you spank your child without discipling him/her through the process, then you are not parenting; you are just being a bully. Gulp.
> ➤ If you only give your child orders without explaining the biblical motivation that should drive their behavior, then you are treating your child like Pavlov's dogs, not as image bearers of Almighty God. Double gulp.
> ➤ If you only correct your child's behavior, then you are not parenting like a Christian. You are, triple gulp, parenting like a pagan.

Discipling your child may involve consequences, including corporal punishment, but Christian discipline should never be dispensed without discipleship as the overarching goal. The only way you can biblically discipline your child is by discipling your child at the same time. The two words are almost synonymous and should be considered that way.

➤ Discipline serves discipleship.
➤ Discipline is a part of discipleship, but it must never stand alone in the Christian home.
➤ Discipline must be administered and received as discipleship, or you are simply not parenting biblically.

Christian parents should NEVER punish their children. Ever. Yes, you may administer the wooden spoon in the discipleship of your child, but spanking should never be administered to punish the child. Jesus already bore the punishment for your child's sins.

Christian parents who punish their children confuse the gospel. If our children think they are being punished for their naughtiness, a.k.a. sins, then they are left to wonder why Jesus died on a Cross. Punishing our children tells them they can atone for their own sins. Oops.

Punishment took place at the Cross, and it has been dealt with completely. Our role as Christian parents is not to whack our kids for crimes committed against us, but to disciple them to love Jesus more.

God does not punish you for your sins; He punished Jesus for your sins. God never blows up and gives you a smack. Yes, God disciplines you, but it is only as a loving Father who seeks your spiritual growth.

> "My son, do not regard lightly the discipline of the Lord,
> nor faint when you are reproved by Him;
> for those whom the Lord *loves* He *disciplines*,
> and He scourges every son whom He receives."
>
> It is for discipline that you endure; God deals with you *as with sons*; for what son is there whom his father does not discipline? . . . Furthermore, we had earthly fathers to discipline us, and we respected them; shall we not *much rather* be subject to the Father of spirits, and live? For they disciplined us for a short time as seemed best to them, but *He disciplines us for our good*, so that we may *share His holiness*. All discipline for the moment seems not to be joyful, but sorrowful; yet to those who have been trained by it, afterwards *it yields* the peaceful fruit of righteousness (Hebrews 12:5–11; emphasis added).

If that is how God disciplines His children, isn't that how we should discipline our children? When we parent our children the way God "parents" us, then we are acting like God. If we do not, then we distort the very essence of our faith.

If we are not parenting biblically, then we will not see the peaceable fruit of righteousness; we will see begrudging compliance until they no longer have to submit to our authority. If we do not play our role as God's representative faithfully, we should not be shocked when our children become untethered.

Permit me to illustrate this life-altering truth with three very common parenting scenarios. You might think this is too cheesy to be true, but I offer you a money-back guarantee on this free advice — if you start talking more like a Christian parent, whose only goal is to increase your child's love and fear of God, your home will never be the same.

Scenario 1

Pagan parenting: Hey, quit hitting your sister or you're going to get a spanking.

Christian parenting: Whoa there, Sport, did I just hear you hit your sister? Then I am very concerned for you. We better sit down privately and talk about this.

I remember when I was your age; I hit a girl named Rhonda and made her cry. Yep, your dear ol' Dad made someone's precious daughter cry. I share that with you to remind you that I am no better than you are; I am a sinner just like you. Let's see if we can figure out why we do such wicked things.

The Bible explains exactly what was going on in our hearts when you and I decided to slug a girl. James 4 tells us that if our desire to get what we want is thwarted, then we murder. That is what you did to your sister. You wanted what you wanted, and when you didn't get it, you didn't kill her, but your attitude was murderous. Not only that, you physically harmed an image-bearer of God.

That is bad enough, but you and I did something even worse. First Peter 3:7 tells us that men are not supposed to hurt women; we are supposed to protect them. That means you committed a triple sin. So did I.

Best I can tell, the people sitting on your bed are two very bad sinners. Maybe we should talk to God about our wicked hearts.

Scenario 2

Pagan parenting: Pipe down back there or I'll turn this car around.

Christian parenting: Hey Gang, I am going to pull over at this gas station so everyone can use the bathroom. Hurry back to the car so we can talk about the rest of our trip.

Did you all wash your hands? Good, but I still want you to use this germ-killer.

While you are passing around the Purell, did I ever tell you about the time that your Dad drove to Chicago with your great grandparents? I thought I was being a perfect angel, but the reality is that I was fidgety and whiny. The police would have understood if my grandparents had left me on the side of the road in Milwaukee.

Do you know why your Pop was such a beast? Because I was only thinking about myself. The reason I acted like a spoiled brat was because I was only loving myself in the moment. In other words, I was being an idolater, and the idol was me.

Maybe you didn't notice, but ever since we left the Ark Encounter, you guys have been really loud. It made it hard for me to concentrate on driving and have a conversation with your Mom. In other words, you were acting the same way your Dad acted on the way to Chicago.

When we act in an inconsiderate way, we tell the people affected by our bad behavior, "I don't care about you. I only care about me." Knowing that Jesus humbled Himself and always put others first, do you think you could be a bit quieter in the back seat?

Now, does anyone want some of this stale licorice I just bought?

Scenario 3

Pagan parenting: Clean your plate. There are children starving in Africa.

Christian parenting: Honey, do you know what food your dad hates? When I was your age, my stepfather made me eat a tomato and it actually made me throw up at the dinner table. I share that disgusting detail because I understand there are some foods that none of us like to eat.

I am looking at your plate and I notice you are barely touching things you normally enjoy. Is there a reason for that? Have your taste buds changed? Did you sneak a treat before dinner?

Maybe you are just a little burned out on mac and cheese. That happens to all of us. So let's do this; while you are eating as much as you can, tell me what foods you really despise and I won't act like my stepfather and force you to eat what you hate.

Please note, in the last scenario there was no theology offered that helped the child love Jesus more. But here is what that Dad didn't do; he didn't make his child angry and resentful. Instead, he modeled the way God deals with us.

As God's representative to your child, forcing him/her to choke down a dish he/she despises isn't really showing the love of God. Conversely, your thoughtful, loving, gentle kindness models the way God treats His children: thoughtfully, lovingly, gently, and kindly.

If these scenarios sound too fantastic for you, I understand. It is much easier to issue commands and demand obedience. Been there, done that. So here are a few thoughts that will help you practice the self-control that this parenting approach demands.

1. Remember that your child is going to go to hell if he/she doesn't understand the gospel and respond rightly in repentance and faith.
2. Remember that you were no better than your child. Your parent's offspring were just as beastly as yours.
3. Remember the joy you experienced when you responded to the gospel. How spectacular would it be to watch your child have the same joy?
4. Remember that God deals very, very, very lovingly with you. All the time.
5. Remember Jesus' promise that He is preparing a place for us (John 14:2). Think of what it will be like to dwell with God and not have your children with you.

Does every encounter with your child have to include a mini-devotion? No, but if you are not regularly discipling your child, then you are not leading them to the Cross. And that is precisely where Jesus wants them.

What about Consequences?

I am not suggesting you become a Bohemian who never gives consequences for naughty behavior. The Bible is clear: if you love your child, you will even lovingly spank your child (Proverbs 3:12, 13:24).

Regardless of the consequence you rightly impose, if you do not sentence your child with a desire to see his/her love for Jesus grow, then you are biffing it.

> ➤ If you yell at your child, you are not parenting; you are sinning.
> ➤ If you only issue orders to your child, you are not acting like Christ; you are acting like a nag or a jerk. Sorry.
> ➤ If you spank your child in anger, you are not being biblical, you are being abusive.

We have all been there; your child does something sinful and you snap. With trembling in your voice you seethe, "Go to your room. I will be up there in a minute." You find your preferred implement, like a spatula or belt, and you charge to their room.

Now imagine this. On your way up the stairs, you stop and remember, "That stupid *Reset for Parents* book said I should only spank my child if I can lovingly discipline him with an eye on growing my child's love for King Jesus."

Do you think that might change the way you enter your child's bedroom?

Call It What It Is

Christian children are never naughty. Yes, you read that right. Christian children are never naughty; Christian children commit sins. Labeling your child's behavior biblically will change the way you engage with your child when there is a ruckus in your home.

When you think your child is simply being a brat, it is easy to scowl, yell, or even hit. But when you remember that your child's conduct is a sin against God, you no longer see bad behavior as something that must be curbed. You will now see your interaction with your child as a rescue mission.

When your child sins, he/she does not need to be yelled at. Your child needs to be taken to the Cross where a sin/forgiveness transaction can take place. Go ahead, try to scream at your child when you are teaching them about Jesus' amazing sacrifice for their sins.

The next time you hear screaming in the other room, before you shout, "Knock it off, or I will give you something to scream about," remember, they are not being naughty; they are sinning. In other words, your parenting is no longer about conformity to your rules, it is about rescuing your child from the wrath of God. This is earnest business.

Typically, we want our kids to stop being naughty for the following reasons:

➤ They are getting up your nose.
➤ You just want some peace and quiet.
➤ You want to do something and they thwart your goals.
➤ You are worried about being embarrassed in public by their bad behavior.

If you begin to see your children as image-bearing sinners who need the gospel applied to their totally depraved hearts, then you will respond to your children's naughtiness differently.

➤ Instead of getting angry, you will be concerned for their spiritual well-being.
➤ Your desire for peace and quiet will be overwhelmed by the desire to help your child understand God's grace better.
➤ You will put your earthly desire behind your heavenly desire to see your child spend eternity with Jesus.
➤ Your embarrassment will diminish because you are on a rescue mission for your child's very soul. Who cares what the servants think when you are on a mission from the King?

Parenting with salvation in view forever changes the way you treat your child. Think of the amazing impact this will have on your little reprobate sinner:

➤ They will stop saying, "Yes, Ma'am" and then do the very thing you commanded them to not do the second they are out of your sight.

➤ They will obey the omnipresent God who never loses sight of them.

➤ They will no longer see your unrighteous anger and have a servile fear of you.

➤ They will not think that God is a simmering pot, ready to boil over.

On the other hand:

➤ They will see the gospel in action.

➤ They will understand the earnestness of salvation.

➤ They will see that you have been affected by God's grace.

➤ They will see you as a loving representative of your loving God.

Is this approach to parenting easy? No way; it demands much of us.

➤ It is one thing to talk about the gospel; it is another thing to live the gospel.

➤ It is one thing to teach your child the gospel; it is another thing to show them the gospel.

➤ It is one thing to sing about the gospel; it is another thing to put the power of the gospel to work in your life and home.

Hard? Yes. Worth it? Absolutely. And here is a bonus for you. If you start learning how to think "gospel" when you parent, God will sanctify you as you focus on your child's justification. You will stop being angry, disgusted, frustrated, annoyed, snarly, and mean. That is a hefty bonus.

Danger, Danger

God has not instructed us to disciple our children so we can have well-behaved kids. God wants to do far more than that in your home. God wants to change children, and He wants to change YOU.

Your home can be one of two places: it can be an endurance marathon with much anger, frustration, and fighting, or it can be a school of character. God wants the latter, not the former.

God wants you to love and appreciate Him to the point where you cannot help but parent with your eye on salvation. The only way that can happen is to first focus on your own salvation.

In order for you to genuinely do any of the things recommended in this book, you must first be affected by your faith. If you simply adopt this book as your latest parenting strategy, then you will have missed the point. You will have missed not just what God wants to reveal to your child, but what He wants to do for you.

Do not read all of the scenarios in this book and think, "That's it! I will memorize those speeches and start preaching them to my kids every time they are naughty." Don't do that.

There are as many parenting scenarios as there are children. You can't give a memorized speech to your child when they sin in their own special way. This is not about parroting another parent. This is about genuinely speaking truth to your child in an effort to help them understand the Savior who has so affected and changed you.

God does not want gospel to be used simply as the latest 1-2-3 Time-out! God wants the gospel to affect radical change in everyone in the home, starting with you, Mom and Dad.

- ➢ Remember what God has done for you.
- ➢ Remember how He bled and died for you.
- ➢ Remember how He rose from the grave for you.
- ➢ Remember how He has provided every temporal blessing for you.

Then approach each combustible situation with one thought: "When I am done, I want my child to love and fear the Lord the same way I do."

Then disciple your child.

That is what the rest of this book is about.

– Reset –

Target your parenting toward salvation, not behavior.

Chapter 2

Show Them the Gospel

When you hear Al Gore or Leonardo DiCaprio preach about man-made global warming, then see them jump onto their carbon-producing private planes to vacation on their carbon-producing private yachts, are you more or less inclined to believe them? Ditto with our kids and the Christian faith.

We undermine our verbal testimony by not exhibiting a visual testimony. When our lives say, "Do as I say, not as I do," it is no wonder so many kids want nothing to do with the faith of their fathers.

> *Dad at church, Sunday, 10:17 am:* "Oh, how I love Jesus, oh, how I love Jesus."
>
> *Dad driving home, Sunday, 11:54 am:* "Did anyone see Ron Hibkins in the lobby? He ate four Krispy Kremes. Four. That guy is such a slob. No wonder his gut hangs down to his knees."
>
> *Dad at home, Sunday, 12:12 pm:* "Zip it, people, this isn't a restaurant. We are going to eat leftovers from last night and I don't care who likes it."
>
> *Mom at home, Sunday, 12:13 pm:* "Sweetheart, do you really think you should talk to us like that?"
>
> *Dad at home, Sunday, 12:13 pm:* "Yeah, right, like you never snap at the kids."

What message is this dear old dad sending? Pop is a hypocrite. Dad sings about loving Jesus on Sunday morning, but by Sunday afternoon, his kids never see or hear about Jesus for a week. They rarely, if ever, see Dad's faith in action. This disconnect leads many children to conclude that a faith that doesn't change anything isn't worth anything.

If you want to help your child understand the goodness of God in Christ, let them see that goodness in you.

➤ Let them see your love for Jesus.
➤ Let them see your need for the Savior.
➤ Let them see that God has changed you.
➤ Let them see how you desire to be obedient to God.

How you behave will either shine a spotlight on the gospel, or it will undermine the gospel. Your choice.

What Does That Look Like?

There are few things worse than being told to behave like a Christian parent without being shown what that looks like. Permit me to share a practical, daily way of living out the gospel in your home.

What you are about to read is not easy. In fact, this is the most difficult thing any human can do, but it may be the most life-altering thing you ever do.

One of the most life-changing biblical concepts you will ever embrace is the need to change your opinion of yourself. Change your opinion of yourself from what it is to what it should be, and your life and home will never be the same.

➤ You will grow in holiness.
➤ Your child will see the gospel in action.
➤ You can say goodbye to most of the fighting in your home.

For a moment, take your eyes off all of the other sinners in your house and focus on you. If you do not currently think that you are hands down, without a doubt, no ifs ands or buts about it, the worst sinner in your home, then you need a radical change of tune.

Don't feel singled out; you are not alone. By nature we are all lovers of self who think we can do no wrong. Let me be the first to admit, I love me some me.

➤ I love my ideas.
➤ I love what I say.
➤ I love my actions.
➤ I love my thoughts.

➢ I love my preferences.

➢ I love virtually everything I do.

That is precisely how we all feel about ourselves. Here's the problem, when you put multiple self-styled colliding egos under one roof, you are gonna have a whole lotta sinning going on. To end these collisions in your home, stop thinking you are spanky, and start to see yourself the way Paul saw himself.

> It is a trustworthy statement, deserving full acceptance, that Christ Jesus came into the world to save sinners, among whom I am *foremost of all*. Yet for this reason I found mercy, *so that* in me as the foremost, Jesus Christ might demonstrate His perfect patience *as an example* for those who would believe in Him for eternal life (1 Timothy 1:15–16; emphasis added).

Paul considered himself the chief of sinners whom God saved so others could SEE the power of the gospel. If your kids never see you acting like a beggar who has been given bread, then they are not seeing the power of the gospel.

Mom and Dad, may I ask you some questions that might sting a bit? Please know that I am guilty of all of the following.

➢ When you sin against your children, do you ever ask for their forgiveness?

➢ When your child sins, do they ever hear an encouraging word from a fellow sinner?

➢ When your children sin against each other, do you force them to "say you're sorry," or do you go to the heart of the issue: sin, forgiveness, and reconciliation?

➢ When the temperature of your house heats up, do you ever put your faith on display by working through issues lovingly and biblically?

If those things are not happening regularly, this is a reason for that: you have an inflated view of yourself. So do I. Change your opinion of yourself and you will change your home.

Turkey Vultures

If you have never been down South, there is a bird that is downright creepy: the turkey vulture. You guessed it — this carrion eater is half turkey and half vulture. This is one seriously ugly bird. Imagine you overheard this conversation between two turkey vultures.

> *Tom the Turkey Vulture:* Larry, you are one ugly turkey vulture.
>
> *Larry the Turkey Vulture:* I'm ugly? Have you looked in a mirror lately? You are the ugly one.
>
> *Tom the Turkey Vulture:* Ha! If I am ugly, then you are hideous.
>
> *Larry the Turkey Vulture:* If I'm hideous, then you are revolting.

That is a ridiculous conversation for two reasons:

1. Turkey vultures can't talk and they rarely name their children Tom or Larry.
2. They are both hideous. To accuse a fellow turkey vulture of being ugly is a lot like two sinners fighting over the other sinner's sins.

My friend, you and I are turkey vultures. We are ugly, horrible sinners. To think we are better than all the other sinners is more preposterous than two turkey vultures fighting over who is more repugnant.

To make matters worse, not only do we not see ourselves as turkey vultures, but we think we are beautiful bald eagles. We simply cannot fathom that anyone could be as amazing as we are. We are self-deceived.

Here is what your children see: Mom and Dad point out the sins in others, but never admit their sins that are clear and obvious to everyone but themselves. In other words, Mom and Dad are acting like Tom and Larry.

This is not to suggest that your feelings can never be hurt by anyone. However, this is to suggest that your response to sins will be radically different when you consider yourself the biggest sinner in the house.

Our Eensy Weensy Pride Problem

You and I are pride monsters, and I can prove it. You and I have pride when we are unkind, act like a know it all, are unable to admit failure, are interruptive, easily offended, constantly in conflicts, demeaning, un-submissive, unaccountable, critical, not willing to delegate (because nobody does it better), won't learn from others (because you already know it all) or welcome correction, don't like to serve, are irritable, impatient, or lack compassion.

It should be clear to all of us that we are the Kings and Queens of our own pride-filled universes. Failure to remember that obvious fact has very bad results:

1. When I have pride, I fight.
2. When I fight, I am experiencing gospel amnesia by forgetting that I am the worst sinner in the house.
3. When I am the King or Queen of my home, church, office, or freeway, I have the right to look down on the serfs.
4. When I have pride, I make a hash of the gospel.

If you had to pick which of those four consequences is the worst, which number would you choose? For my money, number four is the worst. Here's why.

Scenario: Your Christian spouse legitimately sins against you. You respond in one of four ways:

1. You immediately return the volley, only twice as hard.
2. You wait until your spouse does the same thing he/she accused you of, and then boom, you let 'em have it. Even if you have to wait months for your opening.
3. You abandon ship. You leave the house, go to the mall, or work in the yard. You do anything to get away from that annoying sinner.
4. You give your spouse the big chill. You zip it and refuse to talk for days or even weeks.

No matter which form your response takes, they have one thing in common: retaliation. In other words, you are punishing your spouse for his or her sin against you. You are besmirching the gospel (yes, I said besmirching).

Just who exactly was punished for your spouse's sin? That's right, Jesus, the divine Son of God, was brutally punished for your spouse's sins.

When you and I punish our spouses (or children) for their sins, we are basically shaking a fist toward the heavens and shouting, "I know you bruised your beloved Son for my family, but that isn't enough for me. I need my pound of flesh too."

What a hash we make of the gospel when we sin in response to sin. When we punish others for their sins, we confuse our children about grace. When we are dominated by pride, it looks like this.

> You are watching the fourth quarter of a very close game. Your favorite team is in position to score a touchdown and win. At that moment, your child runs screaming through the room, stops in front of the TV, jumps up and down while yelling, "Daaaaaaaad. Jimmy hit me with a sock."

King You thinks he should never be interrupted by a servant. Therefore, you erupt.

> Your kitchen is such a catastrophe you think you might qualify for FEMA relief. Thanks to your toil, you make it look worthy of *Home and Garden Magazine*. Your child, who has a history of letting things slip through her fingers, drops the ketchup bottle. Your spotless kitchen now looks like the side of a bridge in Compton. Queen You can't imagine herself ever being that clumsy. Therefore, you explode more than the bottle of ketchup.

Whatever form our haughtiness takes, we do not act like our Savior when we are not humble.

> Do nothing from selfishness or empty conceit, but with *humility* of mind regard one another as *more important* than yourselves; do not merely look out for your own personal interests, but also for the interests of others. Have this attitude in yourselves which was also in Christ Jesus, who, although He existed in the form of God, did not regard equality with God a thing to be grasped, but emptied Himself, taking the form of a bond-servant, and being made in the likeness of men. Being found in appearance as a man, He humbled Himself by becoming obedient to the point of death, even death on a cross (Philippians 2:3–8; emphasis added).

Jesus never shouted at anyone with sinful anger. Humble Jesus acted like a servant who was silent before His accusers. If you want your child to "see

Jesus," then remember the first message of the gospel: you are a rotten sinner and you have no business lording anything over anyone.

Once you grasp that you are the worst of the worst, you will not yell at your child for interrupting your leisure activity or dirtying your clean kitchen. Instead, we will think, "How can I yell at my child when I am a greater sinner than they will ever be?"

We like to think we are kings and queens, but if we are going to be like Jesus, we need to become the paupers of our homes, churches, and offices. You won't lose respect from your family; you will gain love, because you are acting humbly, like Jesus.

As biblical counselor Rick Thomas likes to say, "Have the same argument every day. Fight over who is the worst sinner in your home and you won't have any other battles."[1]

Ouch

Imagine your favorite celebrity/politician/preacher visited your home. You wake early to prepare a special breakfast for your esteemed guest. On your way to pour fresh-squeezed orange juice for your dignitary, you accidentally step on his foot. What would you do?

Most likely you would beg forgiveness for being so clumsy. I suspect you might fall all over yourself to apologize. That's what I would do.

Now imagine your child shows up, sits down at the table, and you accidentally step on his foot. Would you beg his forgiveness or would you bark at him for having "your big feet in my way?"

Why would you have such a different response? Simple, — you want the celebrity to think as highly of yourself as you do. Worse than that, you esteem the celebrity (and yourself) as more important than your child. Ouch.

When you remember that you are the biggest sinner in your house:

➢ You will "do nothing from selfishness or empty conceit, but with humility of mind regard one another as more important than yourselves" (Philippians 2:3).
➢ You will "give preference to one another in honor" (Romans 12:10).

---

1. Todd Friel and Rick Thomas, *Drive By Marriage*, https://www.amazon.com/Drive-Marriage-Lessons-before-every/dp/0988552760.

> ➤ You will "not be haughty in mind," or "wise in your own esti-
>   mation" (Romans 12:16).

When you remember that you killed Jesus you will not be angry, offended, wounded, hurt, vengeful, or selfish. Instead, you will desire to humble yourself and apologize when you have sinned against your family.

When you remember that nobody has ever done anything as horrific to you as you have done to Jesus, you can respond graciously to your children when they sin. You cannot get exasperated with your child who is a petty thief when you remember you are guilty of high crimes. Here is the bonus: you will be showing the gospel to your children.

The Gospel

To live the gospel, we must always remember the two messages of the gospel:

1. We are really bad, terrible, awful, wicked, wretched sinners.
2. Jesus is a really good, kind, loving, amazing, long-suffering Savior.

Not all, but most fights in our homes, are due to a failure to remember the first message of the gospel. When you forget that you may not be the worst sinner in the world, but you are the worst sinner you know, that is when the fireworks begin. It looks like this:

> ➤ You overhear your child use a swear word. You forget that you
>   too were a child who let bloopers fly. Therefore, you are dis-
>   appointed and angry with your child for being a bigger sinner
>   than you are.
> ➤ Your spouse says something sinful to you. You have forgot-
>   ten that you have committed more sins against God than
>   your spouse could ever commit against you. Therefore, you
>   retaliate.

There is a word to describe thinking that you are not as big a sinner as other people in your home: self-righteousness.

> ➤ The self-righteous are disgusted with people.
> ➤ The self-righteous get angry when anyone sins against them.
> ➤ The self-righteous feel justified in returning a sin for a sin.

➤ The self-righteous believe they should never be inconvenienced or treated poorly.
➤ The self-righteous believe they have every right to brutalize the people who share their last name.

The first message of the gospel should put a stake through the heart of self-righteousness. If you want to your home to be more peaceful, you can stop being self-righteous by doing sin math.

Sin Math

Let's say your spouse sinned against you five times today. Now, consider how many times you have sinned against God today. If you only consider your lack of appropriate gratitude to God, then you have sinned hundreds of times today.

Wait, it gets even more painful. Not only do you sin more against God than anyone has ever sinned against you, but your sins against God are far more egregious than any sins committed against you.

The next time someone sins against you, hear the nails of Jesus rattling in your pockets. Nobody has done anything to you that you have not done to the Savior a million times. Here are some common scenarios and a question that demonstrate sin math.

Your spouse doesn't call you as often as you would like.
Question: How is your prayer life? You don't "pray without ceasing," thus, you don't "call God" nearly as often as you should.

Your spouse harbors a grudge.
Question: Have you spent days, weeks, years, disappointed, frustrated, or unsatisfied with your lot in life? Then you have been holding a grudge against your Sovereign.

Your spouse doesn't say nice things about you.
Question. How is your worship life? We shouldn't just be singing our worship in church; our entire life should be an act of worship. Now, remind me, what were you saying about your spouse?

Your spouse withholds affection.

Question: How often do you tell God you love Him?

Your spouse questions your motives.

Question: Have you never asked God why He is doing something?

Your spouse doesn't help around the house.

Question: How much time do you spend helping at church?

Your spouse never says, "Thank you."

Question: When was the last time you thanked God for air? Health? Clothes? Your house? Your kids? Your job? Your life?

Your spouse spends too much money.

Question: Have you given everything you could to God?

Your spouse tells you that you don't run the house well.

Question: Have you ever complained about world events?

Your spouse says something awful about your family.

Question: Have you ever said anything awful about a member of God's family on your drive home from church?

Focusing on the sheer volume of your sins against God will help you respond better to the few sins committed against you. Hey, I told you this was not going to be easy.

Three Challenges

Challenge #1: The next time your child or spouse sins against you, instead of retaliating, stop, think about your sins, think about your Savior, then engage them. It might sound something like this.

> "Honey, did I ever tell you about the time I told my mother to shut up? Well, I did. Your dad actually told your grandmother to shut up. When I think back to those years, I see that I could be very disrespectful and ungrateful to my mother. I still regret that.
>
> "Your mom told me you sass-mouthed her today. You treated your mother the same way I treated mine. You and I are

two birds of a feather; I sinned against my mom and you sinned against yours. Maybe we should pray together right now and thank God for His mercy. Then you can go talk to Mom."

Challenge #2: The next time you sin against a family member, sit the offended party down and ask to be forgiven. Don't merely say, "I'm sorry." Instead, say, "I am sorry. Will you please forgive me?" That is the position of humility.

One of my favorite authors, Randy Alcorn, recently posted this sweet anecdote. This is especially for you if you think you will lose face if you apologize for your failures.

> Some years ago, I sat with my daughters at a wonderful father/daughter banquet at our church. Someone at the table asked my youngest daughter, Angela, what I'd done that made the biggest impression on her.
>
> She said, "I remember one time when dad was harsh with me. Then a few minutes later he came back into my room, and he cried and asked my forgiveness. I've never forgotten that."
>
> That's what Angie remembered as having the most impact on her — something I had actually done wrong, and then asked her forgiveness for! I thought, *Isn't that interesting?* It shows how being a good example isn't limited to doing great and magnificent things. Sometimes it's when we admit we did wrong things.[2]

You will never be sorry you said, "I'm sorry. Will you please forgive me?" Do not let the offended party simply say, "No problem." Make sure the person you sinned against says, "I forgive you." For the sin transaction to be complete, forgiveness must be requested and granted.

Challenge #3: Ask your family to sit at the table with a piece of paper and a pen. Ask them to write down all of the ways you have failed them, sinned against them, or wounded them. Only a humbled man or woman can do this.

After they hand you reams of paper, start asking for forgiveness and beg them to give it. Your sin-stained home will suddenly be spotless. Then keep your home stainless by doing regular sin-housecleaning. Cleaning a spill is a

---

2. http://www.epm.org/blog/2015/Nov/6/daughter-parenting.

lot easier before time turns it into a permanent stain. When you sin, repent immediately, be forgiven, and your house will remain spotless.

You will not lose power; you will gain respect and love. You will be showing your children that their parents' faith is real and the gospel has power.

> ➤ Show them the gospel has power.
> ➤ Show them that you have been crushed by the weight of your own sin.
> ➤ Show them that you are a man or woman who has been purchased by God and you are under His influence.

Show your children the gospel and you will be showing them something they will desire for themselves. Besides, living the gospel is downright biblical (Philippians 1:27; 1 Peter 2:11–17; John 15:8; Matthew 5:16).

A person must hear the gospel to be saved (Romans 10:17), but seeing the gospel helps a child believe what they hear. Watching a well-lived Christian life does not get anyone saved, but it sure does undergird one's testimony (Matthew 5:16; 1 Peter 2:12). It makes your message attractive and your godly lifestyle "will adorn the doctrine of God our Savior in every respect" (Titus 2:10).

If you want your kids to love the Lord, show them how God's love has affected you. Don't just tell them about your faith, display it. The best way to do that is by applying the gospel to yourself first, and then to your relationships.

– Reset –

If your daily behavior does not tell your children that you are saved, then you are not behaving correctly.

Chapter 3

Have Your Children Submit to the Right Authority

Why should your children chew with their mouths closed, be nice to their siblings, not talk back to their parents, and mow the lawn with straight lines? If we are honest, our answer tends to be, "Because I said so."

This is a classic, and oh so easy, parenting error that has lead to countless cases of apostasy. If we tether our children to us, when they leave the nest, they quickly untether themselves from our rules, our traditions, our patriotism, our everything. It happens every day. On the other hand, if our children are tethered to God and His Word, they learn to submit to the One who doesn't stay home while they go live in a frat house. They learn that God is their ruler for life. They learn lifelong submission to their ultimate authority, not temporary submission to parental authority.

Let's be honest, the favorite Bible verse we Christian parents force our children to memorize is Ephesians 6:1:

> Children, obey your parents *in the Lord*, for this is right (emphasis added).

We love to have our young'uns memorize that verse and remind them "the Bible says you have to obey me." But notice how and why that verse says children should obey: "in the Lord." Those in our charge should obey us as if they are obeying God. Our children's favorite Bible verse teaches the same thing.

> Fathers, do not provoke your children to anger, but bring them up in the discipline and *instruction of the Lord* (Ephesians 6:4; emphasis added).

35

Our instruction to our children should not be, "Do as I say," but, "Do as God says." The next two verses in Ephesians 6 repeat that command.

> Slaves, be obedient to those who are your masters according to the flesh, with fear and trembling, in the sincerity of your heart, *as to Christ*; not by way of eyeservice, as men-pleasers, but *as slaves of Christ*, doing *the will of God* from the heart (Ephesians 6:5–6; emphasis added).

All of us are commanded to submit to authorities, all authorities instituted by God (1 Peter 2:13). That includes:

➤ Government (Romans 13:1–7)
➤ Bosses (Ephesians 6:5–6)
➤ Elders (1 Peter 5:5)
➤ Parents (Ephesians 6:1)

The first and best lesson you can teach your child is obedience. You must explain to them that your authority is on loan from the Lord and you are merely God's representative. They must obey you as if they are submitting to the God you also submit to.

Think of it like this: God has given you the authority to represent Him. He has commanded our children to honor and obey us. They should obey us NOT because we are the authority in their lives; they should obey us because God has given them a commandment to obey us. Children submit to God's authority as they obey God's command to honor us.

If your children are submitting to YOUR authority, then you are concocting a recipe for disaster. Tether your child to you, and odds are they will fly the coup. Tether your child "to Christ," and he/she will submit to Him long after you and I are dead.

This is a very easy line to cross. It is easy to bark, "Because I said so." We must discipline ourselves to respond to our children's "why" questions with a loving, "Because you must submit to God. Just like your mom and dad do." Talk about a radical difference.

We Say Versus God Says

Let's work through some typical conversations that demonstrate the difference between "Because I said so," versus "Thus saith the Lord." We will start with our first four examples at the beginning of this chapter.

Parental submission approach: Chew with your mouth closed, you're making me nuts.

Submission to God approach: Honey, do you remember how Jesus answered the Pharisees when they asked Him what the greatest commandment is? We are to love God with all our might, and love our neighbor as ourselves (Mark 12:30–31). That is why we don't chew ice. Some people get really annoyed when people do that and we love our neighbor when we don't irritate our neighbors.

Parental submission approach: Be nice to your sister or I will teach you a thing or two about being mean.

Submission to God approach: Honey, do you remember when we talked about not chewing ice? We talked about loving our neighbor as ourselves. Do you think you are obeying God's command when you are mean to your sister?

Let me share another verse with you that is pretty scary. Jesus said that if we call our brothers a fool, we are in danger of judgment (Matthew 5:22). Are you sure you want to treat your sister that way, knowing that you are going to be judged by God Himself?

Remember, when we love, we are acting like God because God is love (1 John 4:8). When we love, we are acting like the Trinity that has a profound love relationship among the three persons of the God-head. When we are in peaceful, loving relationships with one another, we reflect the Trinity who is in a peaceful, loving relationship with one another.

Parental submission approach: If I had disobeyed my parents like that, I would have been taken out to the woodshed.

Submission to God approach: Honey, let me share a very important theological term with you: the economic subordination of the Trinitarian Godhead. The Trinity means that God is three persons yet one God. Even though they are all equal, the Son submits to the Father, and the Holy Spirit submits to the Father and the Son.

In order for things to run smoothly, there needs to be leaders and helpers. The reason things work well that way is because that is how heaven operates. The Father leads as the Son and

Holy Spirit follow. There is no disgrace in submission when we know that there is submission in the Trinity.

That is why we have bosses and employees, pastors and sheep, husbands and wives, parents and children. Things only work well when somebody leads and somebody follows. When we fail to submit in the realms of authority that God has instituted, things go very poorly. That is why you have a commandment with a promise (Ephesians 6:3).

God promises that you will live longer and enjoy a good life when you submit to God by obeying your mom and dad. I want a good, long life for you and I am sure you do too. So the next time we tell you to do something, remember that you are really submitting to God who promises safety and a good life.

You also need to remember that when you disobey us, you are not acting like Jesus who always obeyed His parents. I know you don't want to do that, do you?

Parental submission approach: Start mowing those lines straight or I'm gonna mow you.

Submission to God approach: Honey, do you know why God commands us to do church decently and in order (1 Corinthians 14:40)? Because God is an orderly god who is not haphazard or chaotic. He does everything in an orderly way, and if we are going to be like God, then we should cut the grass in an orderly way. When you mow with straight lines, in a sense you are mowing the way God would. Now take a break, and then mow those lines decently and in order, like God.

Notice a Difference?

Do you feel the difference in these two approaches? One encourages submission to us; the other encourages submission to God based on the authority of His Word.

While it is impossible to preach an expository sermon every time our child misbehaves in the middle of Wal-Mart, the overall thrust of our parenting must be grounded in submission to God and His Word. This can be done with EVERYTHING. No, seriously. Everything.

Parental submission approach: Get a job.

Submission to God approach: Honey, do you know what God is doing right now? He is working. God is actively holding the entire universe together by the word of His power (Hebrews 1:3). God is a working God, and His image bearers are supposed to act like Him.

We work because God works, and He has given us works to do which He has prepared for us (Ephesians 2:10). This is why there is dignity in every task we put our hands to. Work, no matter how crummy or filthy the job might be, has grandeur. When we are being lazy, we are not being like God. Now, let's take a look at your options for summer employment.

Parental submission approach: Go change that outfit. No daughter of mine is going out looking like that.

Submission to God approach: Honey, do you remember the first thing Adam and Eve did when they sinned? They tried to cover their shame because of their sin. That tells us nudity is now a sin because we have fallen. That is why Christians dress modestly; it is a reminder that we are fallen, sinful creatures. When you reveal too much flesh for the world to see, you are failing to remember that, and you are sinning.

When we cover our nakedness, we agree with God that we are sinful and need a Savior. In other words, our clothes should actually remind us of Jesus, who robes us in His righteousness (Galatians 3:27). So, do you think a God-glorifier should wear that outfit?

Parental submission approach: Don't lie to me again or I will wash your mouth out with soap.

Submission to God approach: Honey, did you know that there are some things God can't do? For instance, because God is truth (John 1:14), He cannot lie (Titus 1:2). Do you think that you are acting like God when you tell the truth or lie? We want to be people of integrity because we worship the God of integrity. He never lies, and neither should we. Now, why don't you tell me that story again, from the beginning?

Parental submission approach: You better study your math or I will turn into a nun from the 1950s and rap your knuckles until you beg for more algebra problems.

Submission to God approach: Honey, can you tell me who the most intelligent being in the universe is? That's right, God. He is beyond brilliant, and everything He does is intelligent. When we study hard, we are thinking God's thoughts after Him and striving to be intelligent just like Him. As you struggle to focus on those algebra equations, remember that you are becoming more like God as you apply yourself to knowledge.

Here's a math question for you, do you know why two plus two is always four? Evolution teaches that we are here because of random chance. If that were true, then two plus two would equal something different virtually every time. Because God is the constant in the universe, we have constants in math. Because of the doctrine of immutability, which teaches that God never changes (James 1:17), math never changes. When you learn your equations, you are learning to think the way God thinks, in an orderly, consistent fashion. Now, if you need help with those fractions, go talk to your mother.

There is not a single command we utter that should not have its authority grounded in the Word. Every part of our existence has a string connected to God. There is nothing in the human experience that does not find its genesis in God. If it is happening here, it is because it is already happening in heaven.

When we understand that our world reflects a heavenly reality, we should strive to constantly tether our teaching to the Word of God and explain why things are the way they are. That gives purpose and dignity to our lives. That also provides the correct incentive for obedience: to glorify God in everything we do (1 Corinthians 10:31).

If you would like to read more parenting scenarios, please turn to Appendix A. "Submit to me" vs. "Submit to God" scenarios include: worship, education, law-keeping, marriage, and abstinence.

Night and Day

If you think these types of conversations are Mary Poppins-like pie in the sky fantasies, I understand. This approach is radically different than the way we are inclined to parent. If you can discipline yourself to stop demanding compliance from your child, and start teaching them God's statutes diligently, then you will be obeying the most sobering command a parent can hear:

> These words, which I am commanding you today, shall be on your heart. You shall *teach them diligently* to your sons and shall talk of them when you sit in your house and when you walk by the way and when you lie down and when you rise up (Deuteronomy 6:6–7; emphasis added).

There certainly are times when you can simply tell your children to do something. You don't need a three-point alliterated sermon when you ask your son to take out the trash. But if the totality of your parenting is based on submission to you, then start buying Kleenex now. You are going to need them when your child runs off to play in a pigsty.

Not every interaction is going to be a mountaintop experience; sometimes the most thoughtful presentations to our children can be met with stony resistance, or even anger. Don't get discouraged. Just because it looks like you are talking to a cinder block, doesn't mean your instruction isn't sinking in.

Introspection Time

Would you be willing to be reflective for a moment? Which way do you typically parent? Are you the authority in your children's lives, or is God? Have you been tethering your children to you, or the Bible?

One lecture is not going to get the job done. Constantly teach your children about the Lord while you are doing life (Deuteronomy 6:6–7). We parent well when we persistently teach theology to the little ones God has entrusted to us. Tether every command, demand, order, instruction, encouragement, and lesson to God's Word, not you. Work with God, not against Him.

Spanking

This is going to sound radical, but there may be no surer way to motivate your children to sprint away from your authority and rebel against God, than not spanking them when they have sinned.

Your child must learn early and often that a failure to submit to parental authority brings painful consequences. There is a reason for this crucial lesson: receiving a temporary painful earthly consequence is a small picture of the eternally painful consequences of not submitting to God. Spanking is not about unleashing your anger; it is a salvation issue.

You can actually use your children's bad behavior to preach the gospel to them. In a private setting, you can tell your child, "Your behavior was a sin. Holy God is displeased with sin and He has promised to punish all sin. I am about to give you a small taste of that pain. I am going to spank you, then we are going to thank God for sending a Savior who took the pain that should be inflicted on us for eternity."

Sound crazy? I know someone who was saved because her father explained that while disciplining her. Your child could have the same experience.

Permit me to insert this warning: if you bruise your child when you spank him/her, then you are not disciplining, you are abusing. If that describes your experience as a child, I am truly sorry. Please don't let your terrible, sinful experience prevent you from doing a very loving thing for your child through discipline.

Goofs

When a toddler learns to obey mom and dad, he/she is more likely to obey all authorities, and live a law-abiding life. This child is more likely to ultimately submit to God. Consider it your urgent and earnest assignment to lovingly help your children happily obey you because they submit to God.

Unfortunately, you are not going to do this perfectly. What should you do when you goof?

- ➤ When your stack blows, repent to God and your child.
- ➤ When you are sharp tongued, repent to God and your child.
- ➤ When you demand obedience to you without submission to God, repent to God and your child.

Be assured, your many, many failures are forgiven by your loving Savior (1 John 1:9). Then get back in the saddle and parent on!

– Reset –

Even if your children obey you, but do not submit to God, you have accomplished very little.

Chapter 4

Instill the Fear of the Lord

Should your child fear the Lord a little? No, your child should fear the Lord a lot. Most Christian parents protest, "I want my kids to love God, not fear Him." That is understandable, but:

> ➤ Fearing the Lord and loving Him are not mutually exclusive.
> ➤ No person can rightly love the Lord without fearing Him first.
> ➤ No person can rightly believe in God without fearing Him first.
> ➤ The beginning of wisdom is the fear of the Lord (Proverbs 1:7).
> ➤ The Bible teaches 147 times that we are made to fear the Lord.

If we want our kids to love the God we love, then we must help our children have a healthy, biblical fear of the Lord. That raises two questions: what is a biblical fear of God, and how do we help our children get it?

Two Kinds of Fear for Two Kinds of People

When a child is born, he/she is an innocent. Because your children cannot knowingly and willfully rebel against God at a young age, no sin is credited to their accounts. Should they die, they will be safely home with Jesus because God doesn't send humans to hell who have not accumulated a sin debt (Deuteronomy 1:39, 24:16; Isaiah 7:16; Ezekiel 16:4, 21, 18:20; Job 4:11; Jeremiah 19:4; 1 Kings 14:13; Job 3:11–15, 16:19; Ecclesiastes 6:5; 2 Samuel 12:23; Matthew 15:19–20, 18:3–5; Romans 5:13–14; John 3:20, 8:24; Revelation 5:10, 21:8).

Don't ever let anyone tell you that your child who died in the womb (by miscarriage or even abortion) is in hell. They are not. Don't even let someone suggest we don't know where your baby is. We know. The Bible provides 23 verses that make it clear; babies who die go to heaven by God's grace.

Additionally, all people who do not have the mental capacity to knowingly and willfully sin against God also go to heaven when they die. Having said that, once your child reaches a level of accountability, when they understand they are willfully sinning (this age varies for every child), they accumulate a sin debt against God. Frighteningly, it only takes one sin to be found guilty before God (James 2:10; Revelation 21:8). That means, if your child is not in Christ and dies while consciously violating God's will, their eternity is as certain as Judas Iscariot's.

If your child is at their level of accountability and is not a professing Christian, your child should be downright terrified of God. We are talking about shake and quake fear. Like, *A Nightmare on Elm Street* kind of scared.

Your unsaved child is on a collision course with the just judge of all the world. Your child who knows he/she has been sinning will have the same chance of escaping the wrath of God as Genghis Khan. God will give that child exactly what they have earned for themselves. To withhold that information from your child is neither nice nor helpful.

➤ Teach your child that the foundation of His throne is righteousness and justice (Psalm 89:14).
➤ Teach about God's settled anger against sin (Romans 12:19).
➤ Teach your child that it is appointed unto man to die once, and then be he/she will be judged (Hebrews 9:27).
➤ Teach your child that God is a consuming fire (Hebrews 12:29).
➤ Teach your child all of Jesus' vivid descriptions of hell (Matthew 13:42, 50, 25:41, 46; Mark 9:43).
➤ Teach your child that it is God Himself who is going to cast people into eternal, conscious torment (Matthew 10:28).
➤ Read the last three chapters of Revelation together.

You might be thinking, "Yikes, my child is going to be really scared of God if I share all of those verses." I understand, but the reality is, your child is currently singing AC DC's greatest hit. Love demands we let our children know their souls are in desperate peril.

It is not mean to let your children tremble before the throne of God's justice; but whatever you do, don't leave them there. Tell them joyfully of the One who took their place and received the wrath they deserve. Let them know there is an ark of salvation they must run into. Plead with them to fly to Jesus, the only One who can appease the wrath of God for them.

If you teach your little dumpling about the fear of the Lord, your chances of your child singing *Jesus Loves Me, This I Know*, and meaning it, are much higher than if you only teach your child the nice bits about God. Besides, if you do not first teach them the fear of the Lord, you really can't teach them about the love of God.

His love is magnified when we reveal His holiness and righteous anger; followed by the height, width, and depth of His love for us in Christ Jesus (Ephesians 3:18–19). Heaven isn't nearly as enviable when hell isn't preached as a fearful reality.

Even if your child is not at their level of accountability, teaching them the truth about God at a tender age is kindness, not cruelty. And here is a bonus, the child who fears God more, tends to obey his/her parents more (Proverbs 29:17).

It was the fear of the Lord that persuaded Paul to evangelize the lost (2 Corinthians 5:11). If the dreadful fate of the ungodly motivated Paul to witness to strangers, how much more should it motivate us to evangelize our children?

The Second Kind of Fear for the Second Kind of Person

Your professing Christian child should also fear the Lord, but with a different kind of fear than the servile fear of the unbeliever.

> The conclusion, when all has been heard, is: *fear God* and keep His commandments, because this applies to *every person* (Ecclesiastes 12:13; emphasis added).

> . . . but in every nation the man who *fears Him* and does what is right is welcome to Him (Acts 10:35; emphasis added).

> So then, my beloved, just as you have always obeyed, not as in my presence only, but now much more in my absence, work out your salvation with *fear and trembling* (Philippians 2:12; emphasis added).

The fear that is commanded of every believer is NOT:

➢ A horrified fear of God,
➢ A fear that leads one to hide from God, or

> Fear of dying and being judged by God (Luke 12:32; 1 John 3:19).

The fear that is commanded of every believer is:

> A reverential fear
> A fear of fatherly discipline
> A fear that contains a sense of respect, honor, and awe for His glory and holiness.

Our children should fear the Lord without being fearful of the Lord (2 Timothy 1:7). The fruit of this appropriate, balanced, and reverential fear of God is manifold:

> Your child will be safe (Proverbs 14:26).
> Your child will have good understanding (Psalm 111:10).
> Your child will lead a peaceful, contented life (Proverbs 19:23).
> Your child will not fear anything if he/she fears the Lord (Isaiah 41:10; Psalm 56:11).
> Did I mention your child will be more obedient (Proverbs 29:17)?

How?

Helping your child develop a theologically correct fear of the Lord is both easy and hard. It is easy to frighten them with the threatenings of hell; it is a far more difficult task to help them develop a reverential fear of a wrathful, loving God. To that end, do not do the following:

> Hide in their closet at night, then jump out and yell, "If you think this is scary, wait until you get to hell."
> Tell them that God is a very angry god who loves to torture puppies and little children.
> Light a match and tell your child, "I hope you like that odor. You are going to be smelling it a lot when you are swimming in Lake Sulfur.

The correct formula for fear is quite simple: teach your child the Bible. All of it. Simply read the entire Bible with your child and you will automatically be presenting the threatenings of God with the same balance the Bible does.

As you read the stories of wrath and destruction in both Testaments, do not water them down in an effort to keep your child from being frightened. Instruct them that God's anger is resolute, predetermined, and entirely proportionate. Teach your child that God is the same yesterday, today, and forever (Hebrews 13:8).

Don't read the scary stories and ghoulishly chortle, "Muahaha." Explain how appropriate God's attitude is toward rebels. Explain that wrath is in keeping with God's attributes of holiness, justice, and love. Don't paint God as a cosmic meanie.

Don't leave your child in despair; always offer the hope of the Cross. Take them there to see the wrath of an angry God poured out on His Son. Linger there to see the love of the God who sent Jesus to die for sinners.

You will keep your balance if you let the Bible do the balancing for you. Teach the totality of Scripture and you won't fall into the ditch of cherry picking "love verses." Nor will you use the "scary verses" as a cudgel to scare your child into obedience.

As you live life, let their sin serve as a post-it note to remind you to remind them about the consequences of sin. Then, let your concern for their eternal destiny remind you to preach the gospel. Stop seeing their sin as a mere annoyance, but a tangible reminder of your child's need of salvation.

Fear Is Good

From a purely practical standpoint, fear is good.

- ➤ Fear saves us from pain.
- ➤ Fear saves us from danger.
- ➤ Fear saves us from harm or even death.
- ➤ Fear saves us from making unwise decisions.

As valuable as those benefits are, there is a far greater role that fear can play in the life of your child. Teach your child the correct fear of the Lord and you might be saving your child from eternal disaster.

– Reset –

If your children are not afraid to sin, then they do not yet know the fear of the Lord.

Chapter 5

Make Sure They Hear the Correct Gospel

Please don't get mad at me for this question. Do you ever preach the gospel to your children? No, really, think about it. How often do you actually share the good news with the little people you most hope will respond to the gospel?

And not to get too far up your nose, when you do talk about the gospel, are you preaching it accurately? This is something many of us overlook to the detriment of our children's souls.

If you and I do not correctly preach the gospel to our children, we shouldn't be shocked when they deny the gospel. Do not assume your child knows the good news or that their youth group accurately preaches the gospel.

I have asked countless Christian kids at Bible belt universities, "What is the gospel?" Answers range from, "I don't know what you mean," to, "Matthew, Mark, and John."

For the filming of the *Untethered* TV series," I spoke to three-dozen students who claimed to be believers. Two of those Christians were able to explain, "The gospel is the good news that Jesus Christ, God's Son, died for us while we were yet sinning." While 2 out of 36 might be a respectable batting average in baseball, it is hardly a commendable statistic for the Church when it comes to our cornerstone doctrine.

Why?

How have we made such a hash out of the most rudimentary tenant of the Christian faith? Figuring out this answer just might keep us from confusing our own kids about the gospel.

Here is my theory. Within the last 30 years, catechesis went flying out the window when youth group gross-out games proved to be more popular. The result of our diminished theological instruction can be seen in the backslider statistics.

We thought we were doing the kids a favor when we removed Bible memorization and theological instruction — we were wrong. Confusion reigns among Christian millennials. While a tenth grader doesn't need to know if he is supra or infra-lapsarian, a 16-year-old Christian should know that Jesus died for sinners.

Too many modern-day evangelical churches almost get a rash at the thought of teaching children big theological concepts. We demand our children learn big words in chemistry and trigonometry, but we refuse to burden our children with rich theological words like justification, propitiation, and penal substitutionary atonement.

Imagine if your local high school decided to not teach calculus because that word has three syllables. That would be bad enough, but what if the teacher filled the day singing songs and playing ice-breaker games? Welcome to most Evangelical youth groups.

Rather than ditching big words and dumbing down magnificent theological truths, maybe we just need to take the time to EXPLAIN big words. We shouldn't run from theology because it's hard; we should embrace it because it helps us know God better.

Do not let your child spend another day in the dark about the gospel. To neglect this solemn duty has one result: spiritual shipwreck.

What the Gospel Isn't

There is nothing new under the sun; false gospels popped up before the New Testament canon was closed. The Book of Galatians was written to condemn the false gospel of the Judaizers. Since the Resurrection, false teachers have been busy little wolves inventing pseudo-gospels. Unfortunately, an almost-gospel is no gospel at all.

> But even if we, or an angel from heaven, should preach to you a gospel contrary to what we have preached to you, he is to be *accursed!* As we have said before, so I say again now, if any man is preaching to you a gospel contrary to what you received, he is to be *accursed* (Galatians 1:8–9; emphasis added)!

In other words, getting the gospel right is kind of important. Let's take a look at just some of the contemporary quasi-gospels that can make your child accursed.

The Life Enhancement Gospel

The gospel is not a life enhancement program. Jesus didn't die on a Cross to make our circumstances better. This popular gospel aberration sounds like this, "Come to Jesus and:

> ➤ You will be happier.
> ➤ You will have purpose.
> ➤ You will lead a better life.
> ➤ You will have peace and joy.
> ➤ You will live your best life now.
> ➤ You will raise better behaved children.
> ➤ You will get _____."

Countless TV preachers and local pastors mislead millions with the unbiblical offer that promises a bed of roses if their hearers will simply "ask Jesus into their hearts." According to the Bible, the Christian life is presently a bed of thorns with the promise of roses later.

There are five things Jesus promised His followers — trials and tribulation (John 16:33), temptation (Luke 17:1), persecution and hatred (John 15:18–20). Yes, He also promised peace as we live through those difficulties (John 14:27), but He never promised a better life, well-behaved children, or a hefty 401k plan.

Does your child know that he/she can expect life to actually be harder as a Christian? Does your child know that the Christian life is the persecuted life?

> Indeed, *all* who desire to live godly in Christ Jesus will be *persecuted* (2 Timothy 3:12; emphasis added).

Can we tell our kids they will have a peace that surpasses all understanding as a Christian (Philippians 4:7)? You betcha. Can we tell them that life will be trouble-free? No.

> ➤ God does not give us the life we want; He gives us the life we need to make us holy.

➤ God doesn't seek to make us happy nearly as much as He seeks to make us holy.

➤ God didn't send His Son so we can have a better temporal life; He sent Jesus so we can have an unimaginable eternal life.

By all means, let your kids know how holistic the gospel is. Just make sure that they understand that the chief benefit of the gospel is God Himself.

➤ Tell your children they will avoid much heartache if they become a Christian, but don't tell them to get saved so their hearts won't get broken.

➤ Tell your children that they will grow wise if they are in Christ, but don't tell them to trust Jesus so they can become sensible.

➤ Tell your kids that the Christian life has meaning, but do not tell them to believe in order to have purpose.

Instead, tell your children about the holiness of God (Psalm 99:3).

➤ Teach them that He is perfectly pure and righteous (Psalm 145:17).

➤ Educate your children that God is a consuming fire who must and will punish all unrighteousness (Hebrews 12:29; John 25:28–29).

➤ Talk about the just nature of the doctrine of hell (Matthew 25:46).

Then teach your child about him/herself.

➤ Inform your child that they were born in sin (Psalm 51:5) and all of their members are corrupted by sin (Romans 3:9–12).

➤ Help your child grasp that angry thoughts are akin to murder (1 John 3:15), and lust is like adultery in the eyes of the Lord (Matthew 5:27–28).

➤ Enlighten them that they are storing up wrath for the day of wrath every time they disobey you, lie to siblings, covet their friend's electronics, or take God's name in vain.

➤ Remind them that hell is eternal, conscious torment.

Once your child trembles, then share the great news that God became flesh and dwelt among us (John 1:14). Let them see the Savior's spotless life and brutal death to pay for their sins and make them the righteousness of God. Shine a spotlight on the kind, longsuffering Savior who loves them so much He was bruised for their iniquities.

> ➢ Implore them to surrender to Jesus.
> ➢ Encourage them to run to the Savior with repentant faith.
> ➢ Entreat them to humble themselves before the mighty hand of God (1 Peter 5:6).
> ➢ Plead with them to escape the wrath that is to come (1 Thessalonians 1:10) and enjoy the best thing in the universe; God Himself.

Forgiveness of sins is a much better gospel than mere life enhancement.

The Example Gospel

There is an increasingly popular perversion of the gospel that denies the glorious doctrine of penal substitutionary atonement, which declares that God punished Jesus in order to purchase us for Himself.

The Example Gospel actually claims this glorious doctrine of penal substitutionary atonement makes God worse than Adolph Hitler. "How could a loving God actually bruise His only beloved Son?" they ask. Historically, we have rejoiced that Jesus took the wrath we deserve; the Example Gospel makes God a genocidal Nazi.

The Example Gospel teaches that Jesus did not die for the sins of those who would be saved; He merely died as an example for us to follow. This heretical teaching negates the very essence of the gospel. There are at least three problems with the Example Gospel.

1. The Bible doesn't support it. It doesn't even hint at it.
2. The Bible robustly supports penal substitutionary atonement starting in the garden, pictured in the Old Testament sacrificial system, and fulfilled in the death of the "Lamb of God who takes away the sins of the world" (John 1:29).
3. The Example Gospel doesn't make sense. To claim Jesus was crucified as a demonstration of sacrificial love is like a man who intentionally jumps into a raging ocean when nobody is

drowning. That is not an example of love; it is an example of insanity.

Does your child love the doctrine of penal substitutionary atonement? If you fail to explain the glories of our most precious doctrine, they may fall victim to the Example Gospel.

Easy-believism

"Come to Jesus," the preacher pleads, "It's easy to believe." Um, no, it's not. Salvation is free, but it costs us our lives. Nevertheless, easy-believism promises that all you have to do is believe in Jesus and you are good to go.

Wait! It gets worse. Most easy-believers also teach that a person can be a Christian even while he/she swims in a pigsty of sin. The problems abound.

1. Not only is it not easy to believe, it is downright impossible unless God grants repentance and faith (2 Timothy 2:25; Ephesians 2:8–9).
2. Easy-believism ignores 30 verses in the New Testament that teach the necessity of repentance (Mark 1:15, etc.).
3. Easy-believism contradicts Jesus' radical demand to deny ourselves, take up our cross, and follow Jesus (Matthew 16:24).
4. Easy-believism disregards Jesus' demand to practice church discipline on those who continue in a lifestyle of sin (Matthew 18:15–20).
5. Easy-believism forgets that a Christian produces good fruit of the Spirit, not deeds of the flesh (Galatians 5:16–24).
6. The Bible teaches a man is either carnal or Christian; there is no such thing as a carnal Christian (2 Corinthians 5:17).

Easy believer proponents not only dislike the idea of Judgment Day, they claim that God would not approve of those who dare to judge other professing Christians. That statement is as self-refuting as it is un-biblical. Nevertheless, this pseudo-gospel has captured millions. Don't let your child be one of them.

Anonymous Christian View

A growing aberration of the gospel claims that really nice religious people who don't know Jesus will go to heaven. The "anonymous Christian view" claims that people who are trying to be good and worship God as they understand him/her/it, are unwittingly worshiping Jesus.

In other words, if a morally good man is trying to faithfully worship God in the form of a coconut, he is actually worshiping the true and living God; he just doesn't know it. Off the top of my noggin, there are just seven problems with this heretical view:

1. If pagans can go to heaven without hearing the gospel, Jesus' command to go and make disciples of all nations was unnecessary (Matthew 28:19).

2. Paul didn't think the Athenians were going to heaven because they were a religious people (Acts 17), he corrected and evangelized these Greek idolaters.

3. If people can go to heaven without being saved, why does the Bible say that there is "no other name under heaven that has been given among men by which we must be saved" (Acts 4:12)?

4. "Faith comes from hearing and hearing by the word of Christ" (Romans 10:17).

5. Paul grieved that his fellow Jews would perish without knowledge of Jesus (Romans 10:1–5).

6. Romans 10 also tells us that foreign idolaters need to hear a preacher proclaim the gospel in order to get saved (Romans 10:14–15).

7. If idolatry is an acceptable belief, why did God give the first two commandments (Exodus 20:2–3)?

If the anonymous Christian view is true, then all the missionaries who sacrificed their lives to proclaim the gospel to Judea, Samaria, and the outermost parts of the world, died in vain.

Self-esteem Is Not the Gospel

The Self-esteem Gospel teaches that we are so spanky that God just can't help but love us. Apparently we can resist God, but God can't resist us. God loves us because we are oh so loveable.

Knowing how much God loves presumably precious people will give them the self-esteem they need to be content and happy. Where to begin?

1. Self-esteem is not a biblical concept; it is a man-made invention that gained popularity when California psychologists concocted it in the 1980s.
2. Our problem is not that we don't love ourselves enough; our problem is that we love ourselves too much (Matthew 12:31).
3. We are not loveable; we are sinful wretches whom God loves anyway (1 John 4:10).
4. The Self-esteem Gospel ignores repentance, faith, and salvation through Jesus.

Other than that, the Self-esteem Gospel is a wonderful idea.

The Blaise Pascal Gospel

In the 17th century, a Roman Catholic French mathematician diagnosed all humans to have a heart condition. Blaise Pascal claimed we have a God-shaped hole in our hearts. Well, he actually wrote:

> What else does this craving, and this helplessness, proclaim but that there was once in man a true happiness, of which all that now remains is the empty print and trace?
>
> This he tries in vain to fill with everything around him, seeking in things that are not there the help he cannot find in those that are, though none can help, since this infinite abyss can be filled only with an infinite and immutable object; in other words by God himself.[1]

That quote has morphed into the widely echoed, "You have a god-shaped hole in your heart that only Jesus can fill." While there is definitely a grain of truth in Pascal's statement, there is a silo full of problems when we present that truth as the gospel.

It is true that our lives will forever be out of sync when we are not in alignment with God's will, but that is not our primary problem. Our primary problem is not contentment; it is condemnation. We don't simply have a hole in our hearts; we have a blackened, sin-stained heart in desperate need of cleansing (Jeremiah 17:9).

A discontented man who asks Jesus into his heart so the ache will stop, would be better off taking two Tums. We must come to Jesus with a broken

---

1. Blaise Pascal, *Pensees* (New York: Penguin Books, 1966), p. 75.

heart and a contrite spirit that seeks forgiveness, not contentment. The God-shaped hole gospel also ignores other emotions, like guilt, shame, and hopelessness. We don't need a heart filling; we need a heart transplant.

> Let us draw near to God with a *sincere heart* and with the full assurance that faith brings, having our hearts sprinkled to cleanse us from *a guilty conscience* and having our bodies washed with pure water (Hebrews 10:22; NIV; emphasis added).

There is also a practical problem with claiming we have God-shaped holes in our hearts — many people are able to suppress that feeling (Romans 1:18). Some people seem to live their entire lives in full rebellion against God and they just don't recognize a God-shaped hole in their hearts, or in any other organ. They are content and have no need for a heart filling.

Countless people have enjoyed sin for a season all the way to their graves. With the exception of Mick Jagger, people can get some satisfaction from sex, drugs, rock and roll, lavish lifestyles, travel, food, etc.

While Jesus certainly is the only One who can indeed satisfy the inner longings of the human heart, the true gospel deals with our deceitful and desperately wicked hearts (Jeremiah 17:9). What type of heart does your child think he/she has?

Legalism Is Not the Gospel

In addition to the folks who insist salvation requires baptism, speaking in tongues, or performing acts of charity, there is a very sneaky form of legalism that is peddled en masse by smiling preachers who appear to be nice. They are not.

These are the pastors who don't want to hurt people's feelings by opening the law to bring about the knowledge of sin. Without sin, you don't need a Savior. Without a Savior, you don't have Christianity. So what must a false teacher do to stay in business? Abandon gospel preaching for a form of life enhancement gospel with a string attached: a to-do list as long as your arm. It sounds like this:

> ➢ If you want to be happy, then you need to act like this.
> ➢ If you want to be successful, then you need to talk like this.
> ➢ If you want to live the abundant life, you need to think like this.

Word-of-faith preachers claim, "Speak words, and God will obey." The sneaky legalist preaches, "Do what I say, and God will deliver." You could call these teachers "work-of-faith" preachers.

What makes this teaching so odious is that these preachers usually don't say anything blatantly wrong, they just never preach the gospel of grace. Furthermore, they tend to make themselves the star of the sermon, "This has worked for me, and it will work for you, if you do as I do."

This subtle form of legalism turns the Christian life into a rule system of dos and don'ts in order to live a more successful life. That is a yoke, not the gospel. The string attached to this deceptive gospel is actually a chain. Connected to a millstone.

The Love, Love, Love Gospel

A relative newcomer to the quasi-gospel arena is found in the fastest growing sect of Christianity in the world. The New Apostolic Reformation love bombs millions of kids into their circles. They don't twist the gospel; they never preach it. They never preach anything really, except, "Jesus is our lover and we are His romanced bride."

This hyper-allegorized version of Song of Solomon provokes only one response, "Ewwwww." Before we laugh at this ludicrous nonsense, be warned, countless children who need love are falling for this blasphemy. Don't let your child be one of them.

The Fruit Gospel

The error of the fruit gospel is an extremely easy mistake to make. This gospel sounds right because, in part, it is right. But it's not.

While the good news is quite simple, the gospel has many effects. As careful theologians, we need to make sure we do not confuse the gospel with the fruit of the gospel.

- ➤ Christians have hope (Romans 5:5).
- ➤ Christians have eternal life (1 John 5:11–13).
- ➤ Christians are no longer guilty (Romans 8:1).
- ➤ Christians have joy unspeakable (John 15:11).
- ➤ Christians have peace with God (Romans 5:1).
- ➤ Christians have renewed minds (Romans 12:2)
- ➤ Christians have cleansed consciences (Hebrews 10:22).

> Christians have the promise of perfect health in heaven (Isaiah 53:5).

Should we share these magnificent blessings with our kids? Absolutely. But we must be careful to not make the benefits of the gospel the gospel itself.

In other words, we must not replace the fruit of salvation for salvation itself. If we offer the fruits of the gospel as a draw card to salvation, our children will receive neither the gifts nor the Giver. Our children, like everyone else, must come to Jesus because He is the only true and living God who offers everlasting life through the atoning work of Jesus.

Sinners must come to the Savior desiring Him and not merely the gifts He offers. To be clear, a sinner can come to the Savior with the knowledge of all of the wonderful promises of salvation, but if they come seeking those gifts and not the Giver, they will receive neither. Is it possible that your child is confused about this?

Share the benefits of the gospel, but only after you explain the gospel itself. Don't be afraid to cite the benefits of the gospel, just don't make them the gospel or you will create a child who comes to Jesus for the wrong reason. That child will find neither fruit nor forgiveness.

The List Is Almost Endless

The list of gospel perversions goes on and on and on; — the social gospel, the health and wealth gospel, and the name it and claim it gospel. Christians can have a fair number of theologies wrong; the gospel is not one of them.

How can we avoid tumbling into a gospel ditch and taking our children with us? By knowing the true gospel so well that every false gospel immediately smells whiffy.

What Is the Gospel?

In a nutshell, the gospel consists of two very basic messages:

1. We are really bad sinners. All humans are treasonous rebels who hate their sovereign and will do virtually anything to dethrone Him and usurp His kingdom (Romans 8:7).
2. Jesus is an amazing Savior. He is a kind, gentle, loving, sacrificial servant who lays down His life for those who hate Him (John 3:16; 1 John 4:10). Jesus doesn't sort of save sinners, He saves them to the uttermost (Hebrews 7:25).

While that appears to be very simple, the way we explain that simple-sounding message is crucial. Having read countless gospel presentations on church websites, it is shocking how much we tend to assume that people know. Do not make this error with your children.

Be an Etch A Sketch®

Imagine you are a blank slate regarding the Bible. You know absolutely nothing about anything Christian. If I approached you and said, "You are a really bad sinner," you would rightly be offended.

What if I said to you, "God is going to send you to hell." You would undoubtedly think God is horrifyingly mean, and I am a brainwashed jerk who is a throwback to the Middle Ages.

Remember, you know nothing about Jesus, God, or the Bible. How would you respond if I then said, "Jesus died for your sins"? You wouldn't have a clue what that even means. Remember, you are an Etch A Sketch®; you don't even know that Jesus is God.

Children are Etch A Sketches®. They know nothing if we don't teach them. We have a tendency to ASSUME our children know certain things. They don't; they must be instructed.

The gospel will forever be a hash to our children if we don't teach the following five points when we talk about the Cross:

1. The character and nature of God.
2. The character and nature of man.
3. Why God is angry with sinners every day.
4. Why hell is reasonable.
5. Who Jesus Christ is and what He accomplished on earth.

Kindly return to being an Etch A Sketch®. If I took the time to explain the following, might the gospel make more sense to you?

The Bible tells us that God is the Creator and sustainer of the universe. The One who made heaven and earth is perfectly holy. Because God loves what is good and right, He naturally hates what is evil. Because He is just, His character and nature demand that no sinful thing can be in His presence. Furthermore, because He is the just judge of all the earth, He must punish lawbreakers.

Knowing that, let's examine ourselves to see how we might fare on Judgment Day. Have you ever done anything contrary to God's will? Have you ever lied, cheated, stolen, coveted, dishonored your parents, taken God's name in vain? You see, you are like the rest of us — sinful and unclean. Your eternal fate is quite clear, God would be just if He sends you to an eternal prison for breaking His laws.

While you might be inclined to think that is a bit severe, the reason hell is hot, horrible, and eternal is not the spectacular nature of our sins. Our sins condemn us because of the One against whom we have committed those sins.

Because God is the highest, holiest entity in the universe, any crime committed against Him demands eternal punishment. I know what you are thinking, "That is the biggest bummer I have ever heard." I agree with you, going to hell is nobody's idea of fun.

Would you like to hear some good news? God is also rich in mercy and He has made a way for us to be saved from His wrath. God must condemn sinners, but despite our rebellion, He loves us and desires to rescue us.

Perhaps you noticed there is a bit of tension in those two statements. How can God be just and forgiving at the same time? How can God possibly resolve this tension?

The answer is found in Jesus Christ. God's only Son has existed for all eternity as God; but He took on human flesh two thousand years ago for one reason: to satisfy the wrath of God in order to save sinners.

Here's how it works. Unlike us, the God-man Jesus Christ never sinned. He lived a perfectly righteous life and went to the Cross to receive the Father's wrath on our behalf. You and I have broken God's laws; Jesus paid our fine.

> He made Him who knew no sin to be sin *on our behalf*, so that we might become the righteousness of God in Him (2 Corinthians 5:21; emphasis added).

God can forgive sinners because Jesus paid our fine for us. God's wrath has been satisfied because of the work of His Son. We have a human representative who identifies with us. We also have a divine representative who can satisfy the debt that is owed to a holy God.

That is how God resolves the tension between love and justice. Because of Jesus, God can be just and the justifier of those who have faith in Him (Romans 3:26).

Now your Etch A Sketch® is full and the gospel makes sense. Failure to explain any of these five points is to make the gospel downright confusing.

Even worse, you will have a child who never grasps the true gospel because they have never heard it preached in its fullness.

Why do so many kids denounce the gospel? The truth is, they don't deny the true gospel; they simply abandon a pseudo-gospel that has left them bitter, tired, betrayed, disappointed, or angry. Their latter end is worse than the first (2 Peter 2:20).

Do not let that happen to your child. Teach them that justification is a one-time declarative act that proclaims from heaven, "Forgiven and righteous." Teach them that Jesus' act of propitiation can actually bring them back to God. Instruct them that penal substitutionary atonement is not a word to be afraid of, but a truth to be reveled in.

Make sure you preach the back-story of the gospel before you rush to the Cross. If our kids are going to reject the gospel, let it be the true gospel and not an almost-gospel.

– Reset –

If your chief desire is to see your children in heaven, be a precise theologian who rightly and regularly preaches the gospel to them.

Chapter 6

Make Sure You Rightly Apply the Law

Press release: Christian debates atheist association president at National Atheist Convention.

When I received that e-mail almost two decades ago, I knew I had to interview that Christian, whoever he was. I wanted to know what he said to a convention hall full of atheists.

On interview day, I spoke to a man with a moderately thick Kiwi accent. His name was (and still is) Ray Comfort. My first question, "What was your opening attack?"

Ray seemed a bit taken aback. "I asked him if he considered himself to be a good person, of course."

Of course what? That is not what a Christian is supposed to say to an atheist. We are trained to razzle-dazzle them with our knowledge of textual criticism, hammer them with archeological evidence, and then finish them off with a swift, "God has a wonderful plan for our life."

When I asked Ray to explain himself, he gave an answer that explains why so many kids are false converts. "I was opening up the Law for him."

"What do you mean you opened up the law for him?"

Ray responded with a barrage of Bible verses.

➢ The law is a schoolmaster to bring people to Christ (Galatians 3:24).

Paul said, "I would not have come to know sin except through the Law" (Romans 7:7).

➤ Paul also said that the law "killed him" (Romans 7:9–11) so that he could be made born again (John 3:3).

➤ The law silences the mouth of the sinner and makes him or her accountable to God (Romans 3:19–20).

➤ The law is actually embedded in every human conscience (Romans 2:15).

➤ God actually made the law so sinners could understand their sin (1 Timothy 1:8).

➤ If you read the first eight chapters of Romans, you will see that the gospel is very judicial, and we need to usher guilty criminals into God's courtroom and state God's case against them.

A light bulb did not go off for me; a bomb exploded. While I had known that the law should be preached before the gospel, I really didn't know what that meant or understand what that looked like. All of a sudden, I did.

➤ If someone doesn't understand that they are under the wrath of God for violating His commandments, then the Cross is robbed of its meaning.

➤ If someone doesn't comprehend hell, they will never desire heaven.

➤ If we do not "commend ourselves to their consciences" (2 Corinthians 4:1–5), then the gospel remains foolishness to them.

➤ If the mirror of the law is veiled, the sinner will never see himself in truth. He will continue to think like the self-righteous rich young ruler in Mark 10 who thought he had obeyed all of God's laws.

In other words, "You gotta get 'em lost before you can get 'em saved." The law helps the sinner see his/her lost-ness. The gospel reveals how they can be found, forgiven, and cleansed. One cannot stand without the other.

If you approach a stranger and say, "I just paid your fine," the stranger will think you are a goof. And rightly so. But if you approach the stranger and say, "Do you remember when you sped through that hospital zone doing 100 mph? You may have forgotten, but the hospital just released the security camera footage to the police and you have a warrant for your arrest. You owe

$2,200, and you have not paid the fine. But I paid it for you." Suddenly, you are not a goof; you are a hero. That is what the law does.

Imagine a doctor who enters every exam room and immediately blurts, "Good news, take these," as he hands a prescription to the confused patient. People would likely flee for their lives.

Conversely, imagine a doctor who takes tests, gives x-rays, and does blood work before announcing the cure. Upon showing the patient the evidence for a terminal disease, the good doctor announces, "But I have great news. There is a cure." That is how the law works; it helps us understand our need for a cure. It makes the good news, good news indeed.

Tragically, the reason so many Christians do not act like Christ is because they are not actually Christians. The lawless gospel has left our ablest weapon in the closet and produced countless false converts.

We Used to Know This

The use of the law in evangelism has always been understood.

> **Martin Luther said**, "So it is with the work-righteous and the proud unbelievers. Because they do not know the law of God, which is directed against them, it is impossible for them to know their sin. . . . Satan, the god of all dissension, stirreth up daily new sects, and a sect such as teach . . . that men should not be terrified by the law, but gently exhorted by the preaching of the grace of Christ."

> **John Wesley said**, "Before I can preach love, mercy, and grace, I must preach sin, law, and judgment."

> **George Whitfield said**, "That is the reason we have so many 'mushroom' converts, because their stony ground is not plowed up; they have not got a conviction of the law; they are stony-ground hearers."

> **Charles Spurgeon said**, "The law serves a most necessary purpose. They [unbelievers] will never accept grace until they tremble before a just and holy Law."

> **Martyn Lloyd-Jones said**, "The trouble with people who are not seeking for a Savior, and for salvation, is that they do not understand the nature of sin. It is the peculiar function of the law to bring such an understanding to a man's mind and conscience."

Dr. J Gresham Machen said, "A new and more powerful proclamation of [the] law is perhaps the most pressing need of the hour; men would have little difficulty with the gospel if they had only learned the lesson of the law."[1]

Somewhere along the way, we forgot what our ancestors knew, "Evermore, the law must proceed the gospel."[2]

How Did This Happen?

For decades the evangelical church has felt the pressure of a post-modern culture whose favorite Bible verse is, "Judge not." We capitulated to that peer pressure by no longer preaching about sin, righteousness, and judgment. This has most certainly contributed to our 60 to 80 percent youth "backslider" rate.

In the 20th century, theologian Paris Reidhead said, "When 100 years ago earnest scholars decreed that the law had no relationship to the preaching of the gospel, they deprived the Holy Spirit in the area where their influence prevailed of the only instrument with which He had ever armed Himself to prepare sinners for grace."[3]

When we decided to be nice and not preach the laws of God, we found ourselves in a bit of a pickle. You see, if we won't use the law to help people understand they are sinners, atonement becomes unnecessary. Without the law, our gospel offer became, "You've tried sex, drugs, and rock n roll, but none of those things can satisfy. Come to Jesus and you will have:

➤ Purpose
➤ Fulfillment
➤ Your God-shaped hole filled"

If that is the gospel that most people hear, is it any wonder they don't get converted? Sadly, the church is filled with false professors who claim to be possessors of the Christian faith, but their lifestyles betray them. A good tree bears good fruit, not rotten fruit (Matthew 7:16–18).

---

1. Defending. Contending. https://defendingcontending.com/2009/10/15/is-ray-comforts-material-original/.
2. Charles G. Finney, http://www.searchingtogether.org/secret.htm.
3. Defending. Contending. https://defendingcontending.com/2009/10/15/is-ray-comforts-material-original/.

The Law and Gospel Distinction

The law is designed to lead the sinner to Calvary, but no further. The law condemns; the gospel saves. We do not leave people slain by the law, we joyfully give the glorious gospel to heal the wounded sinner. Not only should we preach the gospel, the wondrous Cross should be lifted high so the sinner can see the amazing love of God.

John R.W. Stott said, "We cannot come to Christ to be justified until we have first been to Moses to be condemned. But once we have gone to Moses and acknowledged our sin, guilt, and condemnation, we must not stay there."[4]

If a child is never chased to Sinai before being tenderly led to Calvary, that child is on his/her way to carnality, not Christianity.

- ➤ This child becomes a grace abuser with no fear or concern for the things of God.
- ➤ This child sins that grace might more abound (Romans 6:1).
- ➤ This child's will has never been bent, his emotions affected, or his heart changed.
- ➤ This child is likely to be a prodigal that does the backstroke in the pigsty of sin with no regard for godliness.
- ➤ This child is of the devil (1 John 3:8–9).

What about your child? Have you opened the law for your children? Have you helped them understand that they will not be judged based on the standard of Adolph Hitler, but they will be judged based on God's perfect, righteous, and holy standard?

Have your children ever trembled before a just and holy law? Does your child fear God? Don't make the mistake that countless weeping Christian parents have made: preach the law to your children.

– Reset –

If you have never preached the law to your children, then you have not yet preached the gospel to them either.

---

4. Ibid.

Chapter 7

Don't Lose Your Balance

The Ninja Warrior obstacle course ain't got nothin' on Christianity. To paraphrase Martin Luther, living the Christian life is like a drunken man riding a horse; he falls off one side, climbs back on, and falls off the other side. Christians need better balance than a Wallenda.

Perhaps one of the most precarious balancing acts Christians have is walking the tightrope between the law and the gospel. All of the reformers understood the perilous path of living in liberty while simultaneously striving to obey the law.

Martin Luther, in particular, brought more light and clarity to the subject than any other reformer. He preached, "Virtually the whole of the Scriptures and the understanding of theology depends upon the true understanding of the Law and Gospel."[1]

Luther recognized that if you can't determine the distinction between law and gospel, your Christian life will be a muddle, or non-existent. He was correct.

It isn't just churches that are inclined to fall into this ditch. Parents have the ability to jump into it and never climb back out. This chapter is not about legalism per se; this is about constantly telling our kids what to do, how to think, and how to behave, without incorporating the gospel, thus reducing Christianity to mere obedience.

This is not a critique of Pharisees who create a works based salvation. A Pharisee demands that people follow a set of rules to attain salvation. This is more subtle and deceptive than that. The all law parent/pastor demands compliance without explaining our motivation to be obedient. In other

---

1. Gerhard Ebeling, *Luther: An Introduction to His Thought* (Philadelphia, PA: Fortress Press, 1970), p. 111.

words, Christianity becomes a set of rules by which a child lives. There is no other payoff for obedience other than parents who don't yell at you.

The Law Ditch

If you have ever ordered any of the following without giving the correct motivation for obedience, then you have tumbled into the law-only ditch.

- ➤ Don't cheat
- ➤ Don't swear
- ➤ Don't have sex
- ➤ Don't smoke or drink
- ➤ Do your chores
- ➤ Obey your parents
- ➤ Be nice to your siblings
- ➤ Read your Bible
- ➤ Say your prayers
- ➤ Go to youth group
- ➤ Volunteer at church
- ➤ Put some money in the plate

If these are the only messages our children hear from Christian parents, then we are turning our kids into moralists, not Christians.

This might be a good time to remind you, I am NOT pontificating as the perfect parent. I recognize that on this issue, "I have failed countless times." I learned about the perils of confusing law and gospel after I spoke to many "backslidden" students who confessed that their Christian homes had a scant amount of gospel but truckloads of law. Let's take a look at how this particular ditch presents itself.

> **Law parent:** I can't believe you didn't straighten up your room like I told you to. Now get it cleaned up or you can find another place to live.
>
> **Law and gospel parent:** Honey, let me apologize for sharing a "When I was your age" story, but . . . when I was your age, I had to be reminded constantly to make my bed. What I am trying to say is, I get you. I know how hard it can be to jump out of bed, turn around and make it.

Nevertheless, your Mom and Dad have made a house rule. When you break that rule, you are rebelling against your parents. I know I don't need to remind you of the fifth commandment, but dishonoring us is a sin. Not only that, disobeying your parents puts you in danger.

Do you know what that means? You and I are two rebellious, commandment-breaking sinners. We need grace. We need forgiveness. We need God to intervene and rescue us. Why don't you tell me what John 3:16 says and then these two sinners can talk to God about our sins.

Law parent: Chew with your mouth closed. I don't want to see food after you put it in your mouth.

Law and gospel parent: Honey, do you remember when we talked about chewing ice? We concluded that ice-chewing is not a good way to love our neighbors. Would you agree that chewing with your mouth open is loveless also? Unfortunately, not loving your neighbor is a sin (Mark 12:31).

I sure can relate to that. You have probably noticed that your dad struggles to always love. I can be very selfish and thoughtless. That means you and I are guilty of the same crime; we don't love fellow image bearers the way we have been commanded to.

If I were judged by the standard of perfect love, I would be in big trouble. And it looks like you would be too. Would you like to confess your sins with me by praying to God together?

Law parent: I can't believe you look at pornography. You are a pervert, and no son of mine is going to act like that.

Law and gospel parent: Take a seat, son; I want you to take a look into your father's black heart. There is a temptation common to all men, including your dad; lust is a lifelong battle.

I am certain you remember that Jesus said lust is the same as adultery (Matthew 5:28). I am ashamed to confess, but I have committed adultery in my heart too many times. I'll be honest with you, I am glad I am not a teenager in this age of electronics. I can only imagine how many times I may have given into the temptation to look at forbidden images.

Son, I have seen your computer history. I know that you have given in to this temptation. I understand; the battle is hard, but you have not lost the war. You can have victory over this soul-destroying sin. It's time to put together a plan to help keep you from defeat. I think the best place to start is confessing our sins to God.

Which type of approach do you typically take when confronting your child? If you are a law-only kind of parent, then you have fallen off the horse.

Primed for Anger

Our kids should not be obedient simply because we said so. Our children should happily obey because they have seen the love of God manifest in Christ Jesus. Law-only parenting focuses on obedience while overlooking motivation.

Law-only parenting sort of cleans the outside of the cup, but doesn't concern itself with the inside of the cup. To make Christianity a Pavlovian conditioning system is to set your child up for disaster.

1. They will feel your heavy yoke and never enjoy the light burden that Jesus offers.
2. They will become sneaky and deceitful as they try to please you while inwardly desiring sin.
3. They will grow to hate God as soon as tribulation comes their way. We tell them to not drink, smoke, or have sex, but if a tragedy happens, they will scream at God, "What's the deal? I have been good for you. Where are you when I need you? How could you do this to me? The deal is off."

If you are getting the impression that Christianity is against the law (antinomianism), it is not. The law is good if it is used lawfully (1 Timothy 1:8). Christians love to keep the laws of God (Psalm 119:97). Christians strive to mortify sin (Romans 8:13). Christians deny themselves, pick up their cross and exert every effort to not grieve the Holy Spirit (Ephesians 4:30). What we are talking about here is *motive*.

God is interested in our external conduct, but He is far more concerned with our internal motivation. God has always been about hearts, not mere obedience.

> For *I desire steadfast love* and not sacrifice, the knowledge of God rather than burnt offerings (Hosea 6:6; ESV; emphasis added).

God has no interest in sacrifices or worship from people whose hearts are far from Him (Isaiah 29:13). What does God desire? Obedient servants who love Him and delight in obedience. God wants pure hands and a clean heart (Psalm 24:4) motivated by gratitude and love. God wants our affections.

God doesn't want us to grind out obedience to Him. He wants us to love Him so much that we desire to be obedient. If we persistently preach a rule-based system without the motivation of the gospel, we are not really helping them understand the gospel of grace. We may achieve compliance, but we will not have the joy of watching our children love God the same way we do.

Be careful when you ride the parenting horse. Don't fall off one side or the other. Don't become antinomian, but don't put your children under a yoke either.

Three Kinds of Kids

Persistent lawful parenting can create three types of children who never experience the joy of the Lord.

1. Do-Do-Do Christians

This kid works like crazy and never feels like he/she has done enough. This exhausted child:

> ➤ Never loves enough
> ➤ Never prays enough
> ➤ Never reads enough
> ➤ Never obeys enough
> ➤ Never serves enough
> ➤ Never evangelizes enough

The child who carries these heavy burdens will ultimately buckle under the weight of these laws. Why does a child become a Do-Do-Do Christian? There are many reasons.

1. This child never hears the law applied rightly. They think the law is a set of parental rules, not the moral standards of God by which we will be judged. They do not understand the laws of God are an unattainable

standard that none of us can reach. The law should convict them of sin, righteousness, and judgment, and lead them to their need for a Savior.

If you would like your child to be a grace-loving believer, then stop giving orders and apply the law to their conscience until they cease striving, rest in Jesus, and desire to be obedient.

2. Many children become Do-Do-Doers because they only hear morals-driven preaching. "How to" sermons without the gospel will inevitably create a works-righteous person, or a bitter backslider who is exhausted from performing.

Here is an example of a "how to" sermon. "First Corinthians 13 tells us how to love one another. Love is patient and kind. It doesn't envy or boast. Love overlooks shortcomings. If you want to love like that, then stop criticizing everyone. Stop getting so frustrated about every little thing. Let's be a people who love our neighbors the way we love ourselves."

Here is an example of a law-gospel sermon. "First Corinthians provides a laundry list that describes what true love looks like. Love is patient and kind. It doesn't envy or boast. Love overlooks other's shortcomings. I don't know about you, but I have failed to love people like that. I suspect you have failed too. We need Christ, don't we? We need to have our sins forgiven by someone who lived and loved perfectly. Great news, there is someone who did and we get all of the credit.

3. RADICAL Christian theology can create Do-Do-Do Christians by telling kids they must be totally sold-out for Jesus. It is implied that radical Christians must become missionaries or live a somewhat ascetic lifestyle. This elusive standard does not create joy-filled converts, it heaps unbiblical rules on performance-driven people.

Christianity is radical by its very nature.

> ➤ A radical Christian doesn't look at porn.
> ➤ A radical Christian sacrifices for the sake of their family.
> ➤ A radical Christian serves his/her local church.
> ➤ A radical Christian does not have to move to Bangladesh to love his neighbor.

The man or woman who joyfully serves the Lord where God has planted them is a radical Christian. Genuine Christians live their lives dedicated to God in sickness or health, poverty or wealth.

4. Do-Do-Doers don't hear the gospel enough to remind them that Jesus has accomplished salvation totally, fully, and completely. They do not hear, "Nothing in my hand I bring, but simply to the cross I cling." Instead, they are told, "You better not be naughty." So they try. And try. And try.

Works are the default position of the Do-Do-Do Christian. Life is a perpetual treadmill of works, failure, work harder, fail some more, work even harder, fail again, etc.

While the Do-Do-Doers may look like humble, hard-working servants, these children can actually be quite self-righteous. If a child only hears laws, then he/she gets the message that good behavior can earn God's favor.

This child, like the rest of us, needs to be driven to despair by hearing the law applied in a judicial sense. The law must be opened until they realize they have absolutely no hope in and of themselves. This little worker needs to hear that his works are like filthy rags and cannot atone for a single sin.

Then this child needs to hear what Paul wrote after he despaired of not being able to keep the laws (Romans 7:19). Knowing he was a condemned lawbreaker, Paul preached the gospel to himself!

> *Wretched man* that I am! Who will set me free from the body of this death? Thanks be to God through Jesus Christ our Lord! So then, on the one hand I myself with my mind am serving the law of God, but on the other, with my flesh the law of sin.
>
> Therefore there is now *no condemnation* for those who are in Christ Jesus. For the law of the Spirit of life in Christ Jesus has set you free from the law of sin and of death. For what the Law could not do, weak as it was through the flesh, God did: sending His own Son in the likeness of sinful flesh and as an *offering for sin*, He condemned sin in the flesh, so that the requirement of the Law might be fulfilled in us, who do not walk according to the flesh but according to the Spirit (Romans 7:24–8:4; emphasis added).

Let the law tell your Do-Do-Do Christian that he/she cannot do enough; then let the gospel tell them that Jesus most certainly did do enough. Then instruct them in the ways of righteousness, motivated by so great a salvation.

2. Bruised Reed Christians

The children who get hammered by a constant barrage of rules will inevitably fall into despair the moment he/she realizes they have not done enough. Even worse, they feel crushed when they commit a sin. Their nagging conscience never lets them rest. This is the Bruised Reed Christian.

1. Perhaps this child hears an imbalanced amount of hell-fire preaching. There ain't nothin' wrong with good ol' fashioned fire and brimstone sermons, but a steady diet is bound to drive anyone to despair.

2. The Bruised Reed might be a persistent naval gazer. They take the admonition to examine themselves on occasion (2 Corinthians 13:5), and turn it into a habit. They constantly examine their walk to determine how successful they have been. When they recall how much they sin, they fall into a pit of despair.

3. The Bruised Reed confuses justification and sanctification. They erroneously believe they must continue doing things in order to remain saved. They fail to remember that justification is settled and sanctification is ongoing. When the Bruised Reed doesn't think he/she is doing enough, hello misery.

4. Some Bruised Reeds are simply born that way. They are tender and sensitive by nature, which manifests itself in constant spiritual uncertainty.

The Bruised Reed lives a joyless life. The Bruised Reed never knows they are saved, or they forever lack assurance. This broken and discouraged soul needs to hear the glories of the gospel. A lot.

> For those whom He foreknew, He also predestined to become conformed to the image of His Son, so that He would be the firstborn among many brethren; and these whom He predestined, He also called; and these whom He called, He also justified; and *these whom He justified, He also glorified.*
>
> What then shall we say to these things? If God is for us, who is against us? He who *did not spare* His own Son, but delivered Him over for us all, how will He not also with Him freely give us all things? Who will bring a charge against God's elect? God is the one who justifies; who is the one who condemns? Christ Jesus is He who died, yes, rather who was raised, who is at the right hand of God, who also intercedes for us. *Who will*

separate us from the love of Christ? Will tribulation, or distress, or persecution, or famine, or nakedness, or peril, or sword? Just as it is written,

"For Your sake we are being put to death all day long; We were considered as sheep to be slaughtered."

But in all these things we *overwhelmingly conquer* through Him who loved us. For I am convinced that neither death, nor life, nor angels, nor principalities, nor things present, nor things to come, nor powers, nor height, nor depth, nor any other created thing, will be able to separate us from the love of God, which is in Christ Jesus our Lord (Romans 8:29–39; emphasis added).

The Bruised Reed needs to hear God's Word (and Mom and Dad) declare:

➤ You cannot condemn you.
➤ People cannot condemn you.
➤ The law cannot condemn you.
➤ Your sins cannot condemn you.
➤ The devil cannot condemn you.
➤ Your past cannot condemn you.
➤ Your parents cannot condemn you.
➤ Cool kids at school cannot condemn you.

The Bruised Reed needs the constant reminder that they cannot get themselves lost. This delicate soul must be reminded of God's saving power, and His sustaining power. Remind this child that God is immutable; when He saves you, He does not change His mind.

The Bruised Reed knows he/she can't save himself or herself. The Bruised Reed needs to know and believe that Jesus can. And will. And does.

3. Second Class Christians

Graceless homes create another class of kids that is perhaps the most pitiable of all. This child secretly believes that he/she isn't as Christian as everyone else. They might begrudgingly mumble, "Yeah, I'm forgiven," but it isn't spoken with confidence or joy. This one is a Second Class Christian.

1. This child may have been verbally abused and called the foulest of names. The Second Class Christian tends to believe their abusers more

than the gospel that screams, "I love you. You are mine, and you are precious to Me."

2. This child may think he/she is defective. Perhaps he spent time in jail or a psychiatric hospital. Perhaps she is overweight or poor. Perhaps this is the child of divorce who unconsciously believes that it was their fault.

3. This child may have been adopted and fears abandonment. The gospel needs to tell this orphan, "God is your Father and He never changes His mind and abandons His children. He will never leave you nor forsake you. He adopted you into His family and you are His forever."

4. The Second Class Christian may have committed a big, bad, ugly, terrible, shameful sin, and they just don't believe that God forgives those kinds of transgressions. They don't know that the bigger a sinner God saves, the more glory He gets. They do not accept that God loves to save really bad people.

The Second Class Christian needs to hear the gospel that declares:

➢ God saves rapists.
➢ God saves perverts.
➢ God saves alcoholics.
➢ God saves adulterers.
➢ God saves fornicators.
➢ God saves drug addicts.
➢ God saves homosexuals.
➢ God saves transvestites.
➢ God saves child molesters.
➢ God saves those who have had abortions.
➢ God saves those who are beneath the bottom of the barrel.

Tell them that Paul was complicit to murder. Paul was the "chief of sinners" and God forgave him. Share the categories of sinners God saves in 1 Corinthians 6, then ask if they are the first person in human history that God could not save to the uttermost.

> Or do you not know that the unrighteous will not inherit the kingdom of God? Do not be deceived; neither fornicators, nor idolaters, nor adulterers, nor effeminate, nor homosexuals, nor thieves, nor the covetous, nor drunkards, nor revilers, nor swindlers, will inherit the kingdom of God. *Such were some of you*; but you were *washed*, but you were *sanctified*, but you were

justified in the name of the Lord Jesus Christ and in the Spirit of our God (1 Corinthians 6:9–11; emphasis added).

Let the Second Class Christian know they are loved by God, despite their past. Let this child know that no sin is greater than God's grace.

5. The Second Class Christian may feel like they are not as Christian as everyone else because something horrible was done to them. They were abused or violated. They just can't comprehend how God could love such a soiled creature.

This abused soul needs to hear:

➤ What happened to you was NOT your fault.
➤ God will avenge your abuser.
➤ You did not commit a sin by being assaulted.
➤ You do not disgust God.
➤ The crime committed against you does not relegate you to the outer courts of God's Kingdom. When Jesus saves, He saves totally and completely (Hebrews 7:25). No exceptions.

Let them know that God flips the line around. The people the world esteems as valuable, God dismisses in favor of those who are the most broken and weak (James 2:4).

➤ God loves the poor.
➤ God loves the infirm.
➤ God loves the orphan.
➤ God loves people in wheelchairs.
➤ God loves people who were violated.
➤ God loves people who gorge themselves.
➤ God loves people who starve themselves.
➤ God loves people with mental and emotional challenges.

There are no second-class citizens in God's kingdom. You have the privilege of helping your child know that. Do they?

Rule-keeping Christianity

The dangers of rule-keeping Christianity are endless. We do not discard God's commands, but we must not make Christianity a system of rules. It is the religion, the only religion, that is about grace, grace, grace.

➤ Christianity is the only religion that says, "Good works cannot get you to heaven."
➤ Christianity is the only religion that proclaims, "Your righteous deeds are like filthy rags to God. You can do nothing to rescue yourself. But God can, and God will rescue you, if you humble yourself."
➤ Christianity is the only religion that shouts, "Salvation has been done for you. Now, how do you think you should live?"

Does your child know that?

If God is about the gospel, and He is, then we must be about the gospel too. Our chief responsibility as parents is to encourage our kids why and how to love Jesus more. If we become nothing but law enforcement officials, then we have failed. Wildly.

– Reset –

If you are responsible for creating one of these children, stop it, and rescue them.

Chapter 8

Command Your Child to Repent and Trust

It is not uncommon to meet a Christian who has asked Jesus into his heart, only to have Jesus leave. So the poor soul invites Him back in. Alas, Jesus comes back into his heart, but He leaves again. Wash, rinse, repeat.

Thanks to Charles Finney, evangelicals have concocted countless ways to cajole people into the Kingdom. Finney was the originator of the altar call, emotional manipulation, and decisional regeneration. Finney should have trademarked the phrase, "Make a decision for Jesus," because he invented it, perfected it, and passed it on to us.

Finney did not believe in regeneration; he thought if he could just get someone to make a decision to reorient their lives from bad desires to godly living, they would become good people. We can thank Charles Finney for a cadre of contemporary Christian catch phrases that may elicit a decision, but they will not lead to regeneration.

➤ Just believe
➤ Accept Jesus
➤ Commit to Jesus
➤ Ask Jesus into your heart
➤ Repeat this prayer after me
➤ Make Jesus your Lord and Savior

While these phrases are much loved by Evangelicals, they are inadequate at best to explain the response that God commands from an unregenerate sinner.

If I told you that you can have a pot of gold, but I give you the wrong directions to find it, I will have made you excited, but you will never be rich with bullion. The same thing is true with the gospel.

If I give you the good news, but I don't give you the correct instructions to receive forgiveness, I have not done my job right. Presenting the correct gospel response is just as important as presenting the gospel itself.

The doctor who correctly diagnoses lumbago, and then prescribes 16 ounces of lemon juice, is not a good doctor. The Christian who rightly proclaims the gospel, only to ask the sinner to "try Jesus," is just as guilty of malpractice. Only the consequences are much greater.

The Correct Gospel Response

Jesus' first words in the Gospel of Mark are the words that we should use to invite a sinner to salvation, "Repent and believe in the gospel" (Mark 1:15). If we are instructing sinners in any other way, we are not being biblical and our evangelism could give birth to a stillborn.

The biblical command for salvation is repentance from sin and faith toward the Lord Jesus Christ (Matthew 3:2, 4:17). If we continue to use deficient and inaccurate phrases, we will only create more false converts than we already have.

Repentance

Let's make this personal. Imagine your spouse commits adultery. You have all of the evidence to prove guilt, and you are heartbroken. Your spouse returns to seek forgiveness. What would you expect?

A. Him/her to ask you into their heart?
B. He/she to read a statement written by someone else?
C. He/she to say, "I have decided to be restored to a right relationship with you"?
D. None of the above?

Undoubtedly, you would expect a broken heart and contrite spirit. You would demand a genuine apology and a plea for mercy. You would also expect a promise to never stray again. That is repentance; you would expect it, and so does God.

> Let the wicked *forsake his way* and the unrighteous man his thoughts; and let him *return to the* LORD, and He will have compassion on him, and to our God, for He will abundantly pardon (Isaiah 55:7; emphasis added).

Repentance is not perfection. Repentance is the attitude that says, "Yuck, I hate the things that killed the One who died for me. I don't want filth anymore. I want to live for God."

Repentance cannot earn favor with God, as it is not a good work; it is merely ceasing from sinning. Not sinning is not an act of righteousness. When was the last time you received a reward for not speeding? Besides, repentance is a gift granted from God (2 Timothy 2:25).

Faith

Let's keep it personal. You are standing at the altar when the officiator asks your future spouse, "Do you believe that this person is trustworthy and reliable? Do you believe that this person loves you? Do you believe this is the best person in the world for you?"

Your soon to be bride/groom responds with three yes's. Then he/she walks off the altar without committing to you. Are you happy? No. Neither is God.

If your spouse only affirms good things about you, but refuses to join you in matrimony, you are not married. The same is true for the person who mentally ascents to truths about God, but never fully trusts Him. They may believe in God, but they have not placed their faith in Him.

Biblical faith is total and complete reliance on God. Biblical faith is not:

➤ Believing the Bible
➤ Believing God exists
➤ Going to church on Christmas and Easter
➤ An ability to recite the 1689 London Baptist Confession of Faith

Biblical faith says, "You are my God, and I am your servant. I am placing my eternal trust in you alone. I will rely on you for everything, and faithfully serve you all the days of my life. I am done with me; I now live only for you."

Too Extreme?

Perhaps you are hearing this for the first time. You would be right to ask, "Repentance and faith seems so . . . extreme." Indeed, but listen to the words of Jesus:

> He who loves father or mother more than Me is *not worthy* of Me; and he who loves son or daughter more than Me is *not worthy* of Me (Matthew 10:37; emphasis added).

> If anyone wishes to come after Me, he must *deny himself,* and *take up his cross* and follow Me (Matthew 16:24; emphasis added).

> "The foxes have holes and the birds of the air have nests, but the Son of Man has nowhere to lay His head." And He said to another, "Follow Me." But he said, "Lord, permit me first to go and bury my father." But He said to him, "Allow the *dead to bury their own dead*; but as for you, go and proclaim everywhere the kingdom of God" (Luke 9:58–60; emphasis added).

> Another also said, "I will follow You, Lord; but first permit me to say good-bye to those at home." But Jesus said to him, "No one, after putting his hand to the plow and looking back, *is fit for the kingdom* of God" (Luke 9:61–62; emphasis added).

Jesus was telling His hearers that the person who loves Jesus forsakes and abandons former idols and loves Him more than anything else in the universe. The man who would first take care of family matters or business deals is not fit for the kingdom.

Grace is a gloriously free gift from God, but that doesn't mean salvation doesn't have requirements. God's requirements are repentance and faith, two gifts that He freely gives (2 Timothy 2:25; Ephesians 2:8–9).

You do not need to fear preaching repentance from sin and faith in Jesus Christ. If the law is rightly opened and the Cross is exalted, when the sinner sees Jesus as the single most amazing entity in the universe, the natural response is repentance and faith.

God's Demands Are Logical and Reasonable

Let me take you to a courtroom. The criminal on trial is: you. Your rap sheet is longer than Gordon Lightfoot's *Wreck of the Edmund Fitzgerald*.

- ➤ You are guilty of abuse.
- ➤ You are guilty of murder.
- ➤ You are guilty of treason.
- ➤ You are guilty of embezzlement.
- ➤ You are guilty of lying under oath.
- ➤ You are guilty of robbery and forgery.
- ➤ You are guilty of driving under the influence.

The prosecuting attorney has presented the evidence making it clear to everyone in the courtroom that you are guilty. As the judge prepares to deliver your sentence, your brother walks into the courtroom and says, "Your Honor, the defendant is guilty and deserves the death penalty. If it would please Your Honor, I would like to take his place. Please, execute me on his behalf and let him live. I love him and I am prepared to take his guilt upon myself and satisfy the demands of the court."

That would cause even the most hardened of criminals to soften and gladly give their lives, affections, and devotion to the one who died for him/her. Repentance and faith are not only biblical, they are logical and reasonable.

When we consider that the Prince of Heaven became one of us to die for us while we were cursing Him, there is only one obvious response: a willingness to cease our independent living and live for the One who loves us and died for us.

As marvelous as our courtroom scenario is, the gospel is even better. While Jesus took our place and received the punishment we deserve, we are still in a pinch. Jesus' suffering and death accomplish forgiveness, but we are left with nothing to commend ourselves to God. We offer nothing that should cause God to make us His own beloved children (Romans 3:10).

While it is the death of Jesus that pays for our sins, it is the life of Jesus that commends us to God. The gospel is so amazing that we get credited with having lived HIS righteous life. Not only is the Christian forgiven, we are now seen as the righteousness of God because Jesus' spotless life is credited to our accounts (2 Corinthians 5:21: Romans 3:22).

Think of it like this:

➤ The debtor's bills are paid and the benefactor also deposits a
   gazillion dollars into his account. That is the gospel.
➤ The criminal is not just seen as not guilty, the judge declares
   him/her the citizen of the millennium. That is the gospel.

Jesus' passive obedience on the Cross pays for our sins. Jesus' active obedience to the law credits us with righteousness. Repentance and faith sure
seems like the right response to a God who would do such marvelous things
for criminals.

In light of the glorious truths of the gospel, let's consider some of the
evangelical lingo we may be guilty of using. The inventors of these catch-
phrases were not intentionally trying to deceive people, but these gospel
responses simply fall far short of the biblical command to repent from sins
and trust in Jesus.

1. *Asking Jesus into your heart* might be the single most-used evangelical
phrase in our robust evangelical-lingo dictionary. Does Jesus enter into our
Christian hearts? You bet (Ephesians 3:17), but the question is, how does
He get in there? The answer is: repentance and faith.

2. Does a sinner need to "*make a decision* about Jesus"? Yes, but our
decision does not save us; Jesus saves sinners who repent and place their
trust in Him. If I decide to become a member of a club, but fail to submit
my application, then I will not be accepted and I will not be welcome. If
a person decides to become a Christian but does not submit the required
application of repentance and faith, Jesus will not accept or welcome that
person either.

3. When we tell someone to "*just believe*," we imply that faith is mere
mental ascent. It is not; salvific faith is the faith of a man who puts on
his parachute when the plane's engines stop. Faith is a whole-hearted, total
surrender with no other hope than Jesus Christ. Telling someone to "just
believe" hardly captures that demand. Furthermore, it leaves out the biblical
requirement of repentance.

4. Should we tell people to "*make Jesus their Lord and Savior*"? No. He
already is Lord and Savior and they are living in rebellion to their sovereign.
Jesus cannot be made Lord; He is Lord, and He commands all people everywhere to repent (Acts 17:30).

5. While this may sound biblical, we should not encourage people to *commit to Jesus*. Our God doesn't want a commitment; He demands total surrender, a complete laying down of arms. We don't commit to Jesus, we submit to Him and then He commits to us. That is a much better arrangement.

6. Similarly, we put the cart before the horse when we tell people to "*accept Jesus*." The King does not need the acceptance of the servants, the servants need the acceptance of the King. The gospel screams that Jesus is willing to accept the servants, but we must come to Him seeking His acceptance, not granting ours.

7. Yes, people have been saved who spoke the *sinner's prayer*, but that has happened despite itself, not because of itself. Permit me to explain why the sinner's prayer should be avoided with your child.

Let's say you are the judge of a court case involving a serial murder/rapist/embezzler/con-artist. You order the defendant to step up to the bench and you ask, "Do you have anything to say for yourself?"

Suddenly a lawyer appears behind the criminal and he starts whispering into the lawbreaker's ear. Repeating after the attorney, the criminal mumbles a sentence, "Dear Judge. Pause. I know I am a criminal. Pause. But I want to make you my Lord. Pause." The lawyer whispers one more sentence into the criminal's ear and the thug mutters, "Will you come into my heart?"

As the judge, you wouldn't even offer leniency, let alone dismiss the case. Ditto with God. He is not looking for a parroted prayer; God demands a broken heart and contrite spirit that repents and trusts in Him for mercy.

The sinner's prayer has additional shortcomings. First, it is too often used to affirm a wayward child of their salvation. "Sure, you are acting like a pagan, but you are not. Remember? You asked Jesus into your heart." The only one who can assure someone of his or her salvation is the Holy Spirit (Romans 8:16). Furthermore, the sinner's prayer lacks repentance and faith.

Sure, some people get saved when these phrases are used, but these expressions have also produced untold numbers of false converts. If you do not want your child to become one of those numbers, please clean up your evangelical lingo and teach your child about repentance and faith.

Back to Charles Finney

Charles Finney was credited with national revival because he received so many decisions for Jesus. But the story doesn't end with his evangelistic crusades. After Finney rode his revival circuit, troubling reports began to surface. Christians who had "made decisions" were actually behaving worse than before they made their decisions for Jesus.

A group of concerned Christians decided to figure out why this was happening. They re-rode Finney's revival trail and discovered that he had created countless false converts who made a decision but never repented and trusted Jesus.

The concerned Christians pleaded with these "backsliders" to act like Christians again, only to discover that they were more difficult to persuade than someone who had never "made a decision for Jesus." They labeled these false converts "cold coal." Despite their best efforts, there was nothing they could do to reignite the fire. These cold coal Christians had hardened hearts whose latter end had become worse than the first (2 Peter 2:20).

Charles Finney created a generation of false converts; let us not follow in his footsteps. None of us want our children to be cold coal. If we are to be biblical evangelists with our children, we must inform them that God commands them to repent from their sins and place their trust in His Son.

– Reset –

If you have unwittingly adopted Evangelical salvation lingo, begin immediately to explain repentance and faith to your children.

Chapter 9

Don't Confuse Justification
with Sanctification

Prepare for one of the worst analogies ever. Here goes. Protestants believe that justification and sanctification are like milk and cereal; they go together, but they don't mix. Catholics believe that justification and sanctification get put in a blender and become one big mushy thing. Hey, I warned you.

The Protestant Reformation was fought on many fronts: the papacy, Mariology, praying to saints, indulgences, tradition, the magisterium, transubstantiation, and purgatory. But the mother of all battles was the battle over the doctrine of justification and sanctification.

Rome teaches that works are a part of one's salvation.

> If any one saith, that by *faith alone* the impious is justified; in such wise as to mean, that nothing else is required to co-operate in order to the obtaining the grace of Justification, and that it is not in any way necessary, that he be prepared and disposed by the movement of his own will; *let him be anathema [damned]* (Council of Trent, 1545; Canon 9, emphasis added).

> If any one saith, that justifying faith is nothing else but confidence in the divine mercy which remits sins for Christ's sake; or, that this confidence *alone* is that whereby we are justified; *let him be anathema [damned].* (Council of Trent, 1545; Canon 12, emphasis added).

The Reformers taught that works are the result of salvation.

For all have sinned and fall short of the glory of God, being justified as a *gift by His grace* through the redemption which is in Christ Jesus (Romans 3:23–24; emphasis added).

We maintain that a man is *justified by faith* apart from works of the Law (Romans 3:28; emphasis added).

But when the kindness of God our Savior and His love for mankind appeared, He saved us, *not on the basis of deeds* which we have done in righteousness, but *according to His mercy*, by the washing of regeneration and renewing by the Holy Spirit (Titus 3:4–5; emphasis added).

Rome teaches that many works must be performed by the convert or he/she will not go to heaven.

In order to hopefully merit heaven, the faithful Catholic must be baptized, regularly confess sins and do acts of penance, participate in the seven sacraments of the Church, perform acts of charity/love, and receive last rites.

Since the initiative belongs to God in the order of grace, no one can merit the *initial grace* of forgiveness and justification, at the beginning of conversion. Moved by the Holy Spirit and *by charity*, we can then *merit for ourselves and for others* the graces needed for our sanctification, for the increase of grace and charity, and for *the attainment of eternal life* (emphasis added).[1]

The Reformers taught grace alone, through faith alone, in Jesus Christ alone.

Abraham believed God, and it was *credited to him as righteousness* (Romans 4:3; emphasis added).

Therefore, having been *justified by faith*, we have peace with God through our Lord Jesus Christ (Romans 5:1; emphasis added).

For *by grace you have been saved* through faith; and that not of yourselves, it is the gift of God; *not as a result of works*, so that no one may boast (Ephesians 2:8–9; emphasis added).

---

1. Catechism of the Catholic Church, 2010, http://www.scborromeo.org/ccc/para/2010.htm, cf. also, Roman Catholic Catechism: 846, 1129, 1256, 1405, 1477, 1479, 1498, and many more.

Rome teaches that sacraments make someone holy and the believer must maintain his/her perfect standing through a lifetime of works. This is called infused righteousness. Theopedia does a pithy job of defining Roman Catholic infused righteousness vs. Protestant imputed righteousness:

> **Infused righteousness** refers to the Roman Catholic doctrine of Justification, i.e. right standing before God. Within the Roman Catholic view, Justification is seen as a **"process"** as contrasted to the Protestant view of a **moment-in-time** forensic declaration by God that the sinner is righteous. The instrumental cause of infused righteousness are the sacraments of baptism and penance, whereas the instrumental cause of imputed righteousness is faith.
>
> Roman Catholicism maintains that the righteousness of the saints and of Christ is *gradually "infused"* into the believer through the sacraments. For the Catholic, infused righteousness either gradually dissipates as the believer takes part in worldly sins or is enhanced by good works. If the believer dies without having the fullness of righteousness, coming in part from the last rites, he or she will temporarily spend time in *purgatory* until the sinful status is purged from his or her record.
>
> For the Roman Catholic, the believer is made righteous by *cooperating* with God's grace. For the Protestant, the believer is *declared* righteous when he comes to faith, based on the righteousness of Christ credited (imputed) to him (emphasis added).[2]

There always has been and continues to be an eternal battle between Protestants and Catholics. But there is a justification battle that rages much closer to home: the war for our children. By the droves, Christian children find themselves in a state of perpetual spiritual confusion when parents and churches fail to teach the distinction between justification and sanctification.

When your kids confuse these two doctrines, spiritual shipwreck and bitterness are bound to follow. This error is very common and all too easy to make. Let's examine two slippery slopes we do not want our children to slide down.

---

2. http://www.theopedia.com/infused-righteousness.

The Justification-only Slope

When our children only hear about grace, but never hear about the Christian's responsibility to "work out [his] salvation with fear and trembling" (Philippians 2:12), they quickly become anti-nomian (against the law). They are quick to snap, "Don't be a Pharisee. It's all about that grace, 'bout that grace, no trying."

The convert who believes he/she can go on sinning that grace might more abound (Romans 6:1), willfully neglects sanctification. There is no striving for holiness or mortifying of sin on this slippery slope.

They possess no desire and see no need for spiritual maturity. Sanctification, the goal and desire of every born-again believer, is not on the radar screen of the hyper-graced convert.

This slippery slope has a final destination on its theological downgrade: licentiousness. The person who only hears "there are no dos, only done," easily descends into a sinful lifestyle. The hyper-graced child thinks that he/she can go on sinning because grace is just so . . . gracey.

If we neglect instruction on sanctification and only talk about justification, our kids are likely to become licentious antinomians who love sin and hate holiness.

The Sanctification-only Slope

The slippery slide of imbalanced theology has another slope: legalism. The gospel-free home is laden with rules, rules, rules. The parent who constantly preaches obedience without grace should not be surprised if their children begin to slouch under the heavy yoke they place on their shoulders.

This child becomes a Do-Do-Do Christian. This one is under constant pressure to perform in order to be pleasing to God. But the slope keeps slipping for this child too; the next stop for the rule-laden child is a lack of joy. The heavy-laden performer has no reason to be glad. They don't have time for happiness because they are too busy trying to be perfect. That doesn't put a smile on anyone's face.

The final stop in the decline of the little legalist is: bitterness. It is inevitable that the child who spends years not drinking, smoking, swearing, or fornicating will be confronted with a crisis. Whether it is scholastic failure or the death of a family member, when tragedy strikes, the child who has "done so much for God" feels betrayed by God for not returning the favor.

Avoiding the Ditches

Great news — there are many ways to keep your kids off the slippery slopes of legalism and licentiousness.

1. Put the oxygen mask on yourself first. Before you can help your child understand that the Christian who is justified, strives to be sanctified, we need to personally understand the distinction between justification and sanctification. If we don't have this straight in our own minds, we will almost certainly confuse our children.

2. Grab your child's hand and dive into the fundamental theologies of the faith. Don't skim; take your children to the deep end of the theological pool as quickly and as often as you can.

3. Make sure your church's pulpit is not falling into one of these ditches. This is far more common than it should be. Far too many "Gospel-centered churches" are so gospel focused they neglect sanctification. If your church loves, loves, loves the gospel but never thunders the need for holiness, your child will believe what he hears and end up in a pigsty. The Bible is not afraid to use the words strive, labor, battle, and mortify; our churches shouldn't be either.

4. Watch your mouth and the mouths of your children. What we say and what they say are very, very important. Let me explain.

Watch Your Mouth

We can betray good theology by talking like unbelievers. Have you ever uttered one of these well-worn phrases?

"What's the matter with you?"

The "matter" with our teenagers is that they are redeemed sinners who still sin. They are *simul justus et peccator*: simultaneously sinning, yet justified. When we act amazed that they sin, we not so subtly tell them, "Christians don't sin. We are perfect." To utter a phrase like this is to forget the doctrine of progressive sanctification that teaches Christians still sin.

"I can't believe you did that."

This oft-uttered phrase also suggests that Christians never sin, which is the exact opposite of what the doctrine of sanctification teaches. While we can be disappointed and even grieve that our children sin, we should not be surprised. We should not give them the impression that sinning is not a part of the Christian life.

"Kids these days," and/or, "When I was your age."

Suggesting that kids in the good old days always obeyed their parents is to tell your child many incorrect things.

1. If you sin, you aren't justified.
2. When I was a child, I was perfect.
3. Kids who sin aren't really Christian.

Clearly none of those things are true. To suggest otherwise is to confuse justification and sanctification.

"I'm disgusted with you."

The doctrine of justification disagrees with this assessment of your child. Justification joyfully announces, "God is not disgusted with you, even when you sin."

Watch Their Mouths

Not only do we need to be aware of what we say, we also need to be attuned to our children's words. Does your child ever utter any of these phrases?

"I hate myself."

This child needs to be reminded of the glorious doctrine of justification that argues, "How can you hate yourself when God loves you so profoundly? To hate yourself is to tell God that He is wrong."

"I feel so guilty."

Preach the doctrine of justification to this anguished child. "You might feel guilty, but the doctrine of justification emphatically declares, "You are not guilty."

"I am so embarrassed."

What a joy to tell a child, "The doctrine of justification promises that God is not embarrassed by you. The doctrine of sanctification does not give you license to sin, but it should comfort you to know that sin is not foreign to the Christian."

"I can't pray, go to church, or read my Bible because I have sinned."

Remind this guilt-laden child that the doctrine of justification promises, "If we confess our sins, [God] is faithful and righteous to forgive us our sins and to cleanse us from all unrighteousness" (1 John 1:9). Don't run from God; run to Him. He is the easiest being in the universe to confess your sins to."

Balance

If you have been sensing that I am giving Christians permission to sin, I am not. I am simply saying the same thing as the Apostle John.

> My little children, I am writing these things to you so that you may not sin. And *if anyone sins*, we have an Advocate with the Father, Jesus Christ the righteous (1 John 2:1; emphasis added).

Let's contemporize what John just said.

- ➤ Son, do not have sex under the bleachers. But if you do, you have an Advocate, Jesus Christ, the righteous.
- ➤ Daughter, never take drugs. But if you do, you have an Advocate, Jesus Christ, the righteous.

Child: don't drink, don't smoke, don't speed, don't rob any banks. But if you do, you have an Advocate, Jesus Christ, the righteous. If that sounds like I am saying, "Don't have sex, but if you do, use a condom," I am not. I am only paraphrasing what the Bible teaches. Grace can be dangerous, but that should not cause us to never preach it to the little sinners God has placed in our care.

Sin is not an "if" question, it is a "when" question. Christians fall into sin. It happens; and when it does, we need to keep our balance and neither dismiss their sin, nor make them feel ashamed for their sin.

Celebrating the Christian life of liberty does not give us license to sin; it gives us the desire to not sin. When we inevitably sin, we need to be reminded that the doctrine of justification erases that sin as if it never happened; then we need to be reminded to be holy, not sinful.

- ➤ If you would like to rob your child of the joys of justification, only preach sanctification.
- ➤ If you would like your child to constantly feel miserable about their sins, only preach sanctification.
- ➤ If you would like your child to resent God, only preach sanctification.

Conversely:

- ➤ If you would like your child to resist sanctification, only preach justification.
- ➤ If you would like your child to disdain Christians who strive for holiness, only preach justification.
- ➤ If you would like your child to wallow in a sewer of sin, only preach justification.

If you want your child to have joy and a cheerful desire for holiness, then preach justification and sanctification in equal measures. Do you?

– Reset –

The child who is not resting in justification which motivates their sanctification, is confused about the gospel.

Chapter 10

Prepare Your Child to Meet Other Suitors

Jesus is not a longing boyfriend who yearns to have a girl go on a date with Him. But He is a jealous God who desires that all people love Him (Exodus 34:13). That, after all, is the most loving thing He could possibly command.

That thought makes atheists howl, "Any god that wants to be the center of attention is a mega-maniacal dictator." They couldn't be more wrong.

A generous person does not give a loved one scraps. If we have genuine love for someone, we give them the very best. What is the best that God can give us? Himself. That makes the first two commandments very, very kind (Exodus 20:3–4).

When we love God, we love the best thing: when we love anything else, we love a lesser thing. When our affections are set on earthly pleasures, we are playing in a bathtub when there is an ocean before us. To find our purpose, pleasure, hope, delight, or comfort in anything but God, is to choose table scraps when we could enjoy a banquet.

God lovingly calls, "Stop playing in a cesspool and find true joy in Me." Unfortunately, far too many kids see God as a lot of things (a grandpa in the sky, the Creator, a judge, the one who runs the world), but they rarely see Him as the most valuable thing worth pursuing harder than anything else.

When kids run off to university and hear the siren songs of alcohol, drugs, sex, cheating, and plagiarism, if a student does not already possess something that is superior to partying, he/she will be wooed to pursue sinful things that are fun for a season (Hebrews 11:25).

A child who grows up in a home where Jesus is not made much of, is poised to seek fleshly things that can provide more perceived pleasure. There are two things we should focus on to help our children treasure Jesus.

1. Show your children that Jesus is the best thing they can set their affections on.
2. Show them that seeking sin is like desiring dung (Philippians 3:8), or dog vomit (2 Peter 2:22), or poison (James 3:8; Psalm 140:3), or the stench from an open grave (Romans 3:13; Psalm 5:9). To give our affections to anything but Jesus is to play the whore (Hosea 1:2).

How exactly can we do that? Lots of ways!

Helping Our Kids Treasure Christ

It is wise and good to teach our kids about the wonderful attributes of God: His omnipotence, omniscience, omnipresence, immutability, holiness, compassion, wrath, etc. But the Bible was not written like a systematic theology textbook. The Bible can certainly be systematized, but God wants us to do more than study theology; He wants us to know Him and love Him as we see His attributes in action.

It is wise and good to have our kids memorize Bible verses. It is most excellent to catechize them. But if we want our children to delight in God, we need to take them to His Word and show His attributes at work. This will elevate facts into the realm of reality, which will translate into stirred affections and greater devotion to God.

Think of it like this; if I told you the pancakes at Mickey's Diner in St. Paul were delicious, you would probably nod and file that information in a short-term memory file. But if I took you to Mickey's Diner and ordered a steaming hot stack of the most glorious pancakes you have ever had, two things would happen:

➤ You will have experienced the goodness of Mickey's Diner, not simply been told about it.
➤ You will likely file your experience in a long-term memory file.

If we want our children to experience the goodness of God that lasts for a lifetime, we must take them to the source of that goodness: the Bible.

Permit me to paraphrase Psalm 119:103: God's word is more delightful than Mickey's Diner pancakes. It is not enough to simply tell our kids that, we must bring them to the biblical banquet and have them feast on the Word. Granted, my food metaphors are getting a bit muddled, but you get the point.

- ➢ Telling your child that Jesus died for our sins is helpful. Taking them to the Cross by reading the four gospel accounts of His brutal suffering and death is better.
- ➢ Telling your child that God is loving and compassionate is helpful. Showing your child the healing miracles of Jesus is better.
- ➢ Telling your child that God is in control of history is helpful. Showing your child the glorious return of Jesus is better.

Don't stop teaching theology to your children, just make sure you bring them to the Bible and immerse them in the great stories of Scripture: creation, corruption, the ark, the exodus, the Red Sea parting, wars, and raging prophets. By reading about God, your children will see God's attributes on display as He relentlessly orchestrates reconciliation for His people.

The events found in the Bible are more than history; they are the stories that show all of God's attributes at work in sending His Son to redeem those of us under the Curse of the law (Galatians 4:4). Don't forsake catechizing your child, but don't neglect showing those truths.

- ➢ Do you want your kids to see God's omnipotence? Take them to Genesis 1 and 2 and see a God who speaks everything into existence *ex nihilo*.
- ➢ Do you want your kids to see God's righteous anger? Read Genesis 6–8 and shudder at the destruction of the entire world.
- ➢ Do you want your kids to see God's mercy? Re-read Genesis 6–8 and marvel that God would even save eight souls.
- ➢ Do you want to see God's faithfulness? Read the Books of Nehemiah and Esther and watch God deliver His chosen people from exile and extinction.
- ➢ Do you want to see all of God's attributes in action? Take them to the Cross.

There is no grander way to show your child all of God's attributes on display than when He caused Jesus to be crucified for sinners by sinners (Isaiah 53:10).

> ➤ See God's immutability when He promised a Messiah to Adam and Eve, and never changed His mind (James 1:17).
> ➤ See God's omnipotence as He ordains each and every event in human history to have Jesus born at the exact right time (Acts 2:23).
> ➤ See God's love, righteousness, and justice as He pours out His wrath on Jesus (Romans 3:24–25).

Everything we need to know about God can be seen as we stare at the Savior (John 14:9). Studying Jesus will not just give your child knowledge; it will actually change his/her heart and affections. Studying Jesus will actually transform your child into the likeness of Jesus (2 Corinthians 3:18).

Pre-Cross Jesus

You don't have to wait until the New Testament to get to the Cross; you can travel through the Old Testament with your children and point them to Jesus Christ along the way.

Jesus did not burst onto the scene in the Gospel of Matthew; Jesus was present and promised in the beginning. As soon as Adam and Eve sinned, God promised one who would crush the serpent's head (Genesis 3:15). God made a covenant with Abraham that the Messiah would come from Abraham's loins (Genesis 22:18; Galatians 3:16).

The rest of the Old Testament is the history of God fulfilling those promises. Along the way, God is not silent about Jesus.

Jesus told the Pharisees that the books of Moses testify about Him (John 5:39). Jesus taught two disciples about Himself from every book in the Old Testament (Luke 24:27). Paul reasoned with the Jews about Jesus from the Old Testament Scriptures (Acts 17:2). If you fail to look for Jesus, you won't find Him. But if you rightly read the Old Testament, you will see Him everywhere.

Colossians 2:16–17 tells us that actual people, places, things, and events in the Old Testament were lesser pictures of a greater reality: Jesus Christ. God was persistently pointing to Jesus throughout the history of the Old Testament by painting fuzzy pictures of Jesus:

➤ The ark was a picture of Jesus (1 Peter 3:18–22).

➤ The ladder Jacob saw was a picture of Jesus (Genesis 28:12; John 1:51).

➤ The Jewish exodus out of Egypt was a picture of Jesus (Matthew 2:13–15).

➤ The manna and water in the wilderness were pictures of Jesus (John 6:36; 1 Corinthians 10:4).

➤ The bronze serpent was a picture of Jesus (John 3:14–15).

➤ The entire sacrificial system was a picture of Jesus (Hebrews 10:10).

➤ The millions of slain lambs were pictures of Jesus (John 1:29).

➤ The Sabbath rest was a picture of the eternal rest we have in Jesus (Mark 2:28; Hebrews 4:9–11).

➤ The concept of surety was a picture of Jesus (Genesis 43:9, 44:32–34; Hebrews 7:22).

➤ The festivals were fuzzy pictures of Jesus (Colossians 2:16–17).

➤ The cities of refuge were pictures of Jesus (Numbers 35:9–15; Hebrews 6:18).

➤ The tabernacle was a picture of Jesus (Matthew 12:6; Hebrews 8–10).

➤ The furniture in the tabernacle was a picture of Jesus (Hebrews 8–10).

➤ The offices of prophet, priest (1 Samuel 2:35–36; Hebrews 7:23–24, 9:11–12), and king (2 Samuel 7:12–16; Matthew 2:2; John 1:49) were pictures of Jesus.

➤ Abel (Genesis 4:1–5; Hebrews 11:4, 12:24), Melchizedek (Hebrews 6:17–20, 7:1–17), Isaac (Genesis 22:1–13), Moses (Deuteronomy 18:15; Acts 7:37), Jonah (Matthew 12:39), Solomon (Matthew 12:42), Boaz (Ruth 3:1–8; Matthew 1:21; Hebrews 2:14–15, 9:12), and David (2 Samuel 7:12) were pictures of Jesus.

Your children can learn much about Jesus from the Old Testament.

> He is a better man than Adam.
> He is a better preacher than Abel.

He is a better priest than Melchizedek.

He is a better contender than Jacob.

He is a better ruler than King David.

He is wiser than Solomon.

Jesus is the supreme prophet.

Jesus is the supreme high priest.

Jesus is the supreme king.

He is the serpent raised up for us.

He is the ark of our salvation.

He is the only door of salvation.

He is the ladder who takes us to heaven.

He is our city of refuge.

Jesus is our surety and our Sabbath rest.

Jesus is the bread of life.

Jesus is the living water.

He is our bridegroom and brother.

He is our Rock, our Fortress, and our Deliverer.

He is our Savior and our ransom.

He is the Holy One of Israel, and He is our God.

Don't bypass the Old Testament to get to Jesus in the New Testament. Show them the majesty of God, in Christ, starting in the Book of Genesis.

For a very thorough treatment of the Old Testament pictures of Christ, lead your children through the "Jesus Unmasked Bible Study."[1] They will see that Jesus is the star of the Old Testament, and God was preaching the gospel to the world long before Jesus died on a Cross.

Cross

Isaac Watts was spot on: when we survey the wondrous Cross on which the Prince of Glory died, everything we own pales by comparison. The Cross is the zenith of the Bible and it is there we best see God's wrath and goodness on display.

If you want your kids to understand the love and holiness of God, bring them to the Cross where they can see love and righteousness collide. God is so holy, only the death of His only beloved Son could satisfy His wrath. God is so loving, He didn't merely permit the death of Jesus, He

---

1. This is a workbook we published and it is available at www.wretched.tv.

orchestrated every single detail of the violent death of His only beloved Son (Acts 4:28).

- ➤ Have your children heard the lashes that the Prince of Peace received as the cat-o-nine tales shredded His back?
- ➤ Have they heard the sickening thud of the punches that landed squarely on the Lord of Glory's face?
- ➤ Have they heard the staff that was repeatedly applied to the skull of the Light of the World?
- ➤ Have they felt the spit that splattered the Diamond of Heaven?
- ➤ Do they know their God was stripped naked and mocked by the very creatures He created to be His image bearers?
- ➤ Have you shown your child the tender area of the wrist where nails were hammered through the hands of the carpenter of Galilee?
- ➤ Have you shown your kids the tender area of the Achilles heel where nails were driven through the feet of the One who walked on water?
- ➤ Have they heard King Jesus gasping for breath until He died from suffocation?

Bring your child to the Cross regularly and camp under the pierced feet of Jesus. Look up at the bloody man who hangs there. Let your children know, in vivid detail, what God did to set them free. Don't just tell them, show them the love of God (1 John 4:10). Like John the Baptist, encourage your children to behold Jesus Christ, the Lamb of God who takes away the sins of the world (John 1:29).

Post-Cross

The reverberations from the Cross have not ceased. The work that Jesus accomplished on behalf of sinners echoes to this day. Does your child know everything that was won for them by Jesus? Have they been awed at the effects of the gospel? Here are just a dozen things that God does for us because of the Cross.

1. God reconciles us to Himself (2 Corinthians 5:17–19).
2. God moves us from spiritual death to life (John 3:1–8).
3. God justifies us, declaring us, "Not guilty" (Romans 5:1–9).

4. God redeems us, buying us out of slavery to sin and the devil (1 Peter 1:18–19).

5. God forgives all of our sins — past, present, and future (Colossians 2:14; Ephesians 1:7).

6. God cleanses us and removes the stain of sin (Hebrews 9:14).

7. God sanctifies us and makes us holy, set apart for a special purpose (1 Corinthians 1:2, 30)

8. God seals us with His Spirit to guarantee your glorification (Ephesians 1:13).

9. God gives us His Spirit to indwell and empower us (Romans 8:9).

10. God brings us into His family as a beloved child (Romans 8:14–17).

11. God grants us eternal life (John 11:25–27) and makes us heirs (Romans 8:17) with an eternal inheritance (1 Peter 1:3–4).

12. God declares us saints (Colossians 1:2), prepares a place for us (John 14:2), and allows us to reign with Him (2 Timothy 2:12).

All of that and much more is ours because of Jesus. Do your kids know these precious promises? Do they know that the Cross offers much more than forgiveness of sins? Do they know the precious promises that are provided in the Cross? Do they love Jesus because of His amazing grace?

Music, Music, Music

One of the easiest ways to saturate your child's brain with the goodness of God is through sound and balanced worship music. Most of us find it easier to remember lyrics than to memorize Bible verses. Be honest, depending on your age, you remember the contemporary hits from your youth. Wanna bet? See how many lines you know from a few of the top ten hits of the last 50 years:

➤ "Hey Jude" by the Beatles
➤ "You Light up My Life" by Debbie Boone
➤ "Endless Love" by Dianna Ross and Lionel Ritchie
➤ "Hound Dog" by Elvis Presley
➤ "Everything I Do, I Do It for You" by Bryan Adams

While I can't remember every single line, I can still remember lyrics from songs I actually hated as a child. If forced, I could sing most of "Crocodile Rock," "Love Will Keep Us Together," and "How Deep Is Your Love." Music is a powerful instruction tool.

In the fourth century, the heretic Arius wrote little ditties that grew in popularity and spread his false teaching far and wide. Here is just one example from his Heresy Hymnal:

> Although the Son did not exist, the Father was still God.
> Hence the Son, not being eternal came into existence by
> the Father's will.[2]

If Arius had won the day, Trinitarians would be heretics today. Arius almost did win the day, thanks in large part to his widespread use of music.

Do you know what kind of Christian music your children listen to? Have you pondered the danger of its imbalanced content? Here is a stanza from two popular worship songs for youth. The first was written in the 21st century:

> So heaven meets earth like a sloppy wet kiss
> And my heart turns violently inside of my chest
> I don't have time to maintain these regrets
> When I think about the way
> That he loves us
> Oh how He loves us
> Oh how He loves us
> How He loves us so.[3]

The following stanza was written for a children's hymnal by Isaac Watts in the 18th century.

> In heaven he shines with beams of love,
> With wrath in hell beneath:

---

2. http://www.johnsanidopoulos.com/2011/06/poisonous-songs-of-arius.html.
3. John Mark McMillan, "How He Loves," https://www.google.com/webhp?sourceid=chrome-instant&ion=1&espv=2&ie=UTF-8#q=john+mark+mcmillan+how+he+loves+lyrics&stick=H4sIAAAAAAAAAONgecSYyC3w8sc9YamISWtOXmMM4lLKTrbSzy0tzkzWL0pNzi9KycxLj0_OKS0uSS2yyqksykwuFtLhYnPNK8ksqRRS4hKQ4tFP1zcsNjAtKEvKqdJgkOLjQhHhAQAm0PulZgAAAA.

> 'Tis on his earth I stand or move,
> And 'tis his air I breathe.[4]

It's funny, but that particular verse of the Watts' hymn can't be found in any hymnal today. What a shame. Watts balanced God's love and wrath in a single sentence. That is the type of balance your child's music should possess.

Don't get me wrong, it is swell to sing about God's love. But if that is all our children sing about, then they will not understand how awesome and multi-faceted God is.

Make sure your kids are not constantly consuming candy. Make sure their music is meaty.

Puny vs. Powerful Prayers

You could start the day with your kids by praying this prayer:

> Dear Lord. Thank You for this day. Help us to glorify You in everything we do. Please protect us while we are apart, and bring us back together safely tonight. Amen.

Or, you could pray a morning prayer the way the Puritans did:

> O God, the author of all good, I come to Thee for the grace another day will require for its duties and events. I step out into a wicked world; I carry about with me an evil heart. I know that without Thee I can do nothing, that everything with which I shall be concerned, however harmless in itself, may prove an occasion of sin or folly, unless I am kept by Thy power. Hold Thou me up and I shall be safe.
>
> Preserve my understanding from subtlety of error, my affections from love of idols, my character from stain of vice, my profession from every form of evil. May I engage in nothing in which I cannot implore Thy blessing, and in which I cannot invite Thy inspection. Prosper me in all lawful undertakings, or prepare me for disappointments. Give me neither poverty nor riches. Feed me with food convenient for me, lest I be full and deny Thee and say, Who is the Lord? or be poor, and steal, and take Thy name in vain.

---

4. http://fullonlinebook.com/poems/praise-for-creation-and-providence/tdby.html.

> Teach me how to use the world and not abuse it, to improve my talents, to redeem my time, to walk in wisdom toward those without, and in kindness to those within, to do good to all men, and especially to my fellow Christians. And to Thee be the glory.[5]

So, which prayer do you suppose would most help your child to love the Lord more?

Fury Not in God

There is something else you can do to help your child treasure Christ and reject idols; — you can expose them to strong, biblical preaching.

A puritan once preached a sermon titled, "Fury Not in God." That does not mean God doesn't pour out His wrath in furious anger, but that He is not a perpetually furious God. In other words, He is not a simmering 211-degree pot of water ready to boil over. God is not a fuming father; His anger is settled, resolved, and totally under control.

God is not ready to fly off the handle and happily hurl people to hell. God will cast people to hell, but He doesn't shout, "Whoop-de-doo," while He flings them there. Furthermore, God does not prefer damnation; God prefers something far grander: salvation.

Here are some snippets from the sermon, "Fury Not in God,"[6] based on Isaiah 27:4–5, which demonstrates the correct balance between the wrath of God and the grace of God. This is the type of preaching that leads a child to stand amazed at His grace.

> On the last day there will be a tremendous discharge of fury. That wrath which sinners are now doing so much to treasure up will all be poured forth on them. . . . Oh, my brethren, that God who is grieved and who is angry with sinners every day, will in the last day pour it all forth in one mighty torrent on the heads of the impenitent. It is now gathering and accumulating in a storehouse of vengeance. . . . and when time shall be no more, will the door of this storehouse will be opened, that the fury of the Lord may break loose upon the guilty and accomplish upon them the weight and the terror of all His threatenings.

---

5. http://www.oldlandmarks.com/puritan.htm.
6. Thomas Chalmers, "Fury Not in God," http://www.chapellibrary.org/files/4613/7643/3208/fnig.pdf.

. . . the earth shall be burned up, and the heavens shall be dissolved, and the elements shall melt with fervent heat, and the Lord Jesus shall be revealed from heaven with His mighty angels, in flaming fire, taking vengeance on those who know not God, and obey not the gospel of our Lord Jesus Christ; and they shall be punished with everlasting destruction from the presence of the Lord, and from the glory of His power.

Before we continue, may I ask you — when was the last time your child heard a sermon that sounded even a little like this? When was the last time your family heard about the wrath of God? When was the last time you heard a sermon that made your children fear God?

Old dead guys used to preach like this all the time. Our forefathers made much of hell, because in doing so, they made much of God's goodness in saving hell-bound sinners.

- When we water down theology, we water down God.
- When we use words like mistakes, regrets, and messy lives to describe sin, we make hell sound unreasonable and downright cruel.
- When we rush past the doctrine of hell in order to get people to heaven, we only end up populating the former while making the latter undesirable.
- When we make God sound like the eternal Good Humor Man, we rob people of the joy of His salvation.

And now, back to the dead puritan preacher.

He speaks of the ease with which He could accomplish His wrath upon His enemies. They would perish before Him like the moth. . . . God is saying in the text that this is not what He is wanting. . . . The glory He would achieve by a victory over a host so feeble is not a glory that His heart is at all set upon.

Oh, no! ye children of men. He has no pleasure in your death; He is not seeking to magnify Himself by the destruction of so paltry a foe; He could devour you in a moment; He could burn you up like stubble; and you mistake it if you think that renown on so poor a field of contest is a renown that He is at all aspiring after.

Did this Puritan preacher talk about wrath and hell? Yes and yes. But preachers of old never said, "Amen," without sharing the good news too.

> Who would set the grasshoppers in battle array against the giants? Who would set thorns and briers in battle array against God? This is not what He wants: He would rather something else. Be assured, He would rather you were to turn, and to live, and to come into His vineyard, and submit to the regenerating power of His spiritual husbandry, and be changed from the nature of an accursed plant to a tree of righteousness. . . .

> It is true that by your death He could manifest the dignity of His Godhead; He could make known the power of His wrath. . . . But He does not want to magnify Himself over men in this way; He has no ambition whatever after the renown of such a victory, over such weak and insignificant enemies. . . .

> And so in Scripture everywhere do we see Him pleading and protesting with you that He does not want to signalize Himself upon the ruin of any, but would rather that they should turn and be saved.

Take a breath. That is some seriously earnest preaching. Now this puritan is going to make a shocking statement that makes most evangelicals blanch.

> He will be glorified in the destruction of the sinner, but He would like better to be glorified by his salvation. To destroy you is to do no more than to set fire to briers and thorns, and to consume them; but to save you — this is indeed the power of God and the wisdom of God — this is the mighty achievement which angels desire to look into — this is the enterprise upon which a mighty Captain embarked all the energy that belonged to Him, and traveled in the greatness of His strength until that He accomplished it. . . .

> He does not want to enter into the battle with you, or to consume you like stubble by the breath of His indignation. No, He wants to transform sinners into saints: He wants to transform vessels of wrath into vessels of mercy, and to make known the riches of His glory on those whom He had afore prepared unto glory. . . .

From enemies to make friends of you; from the children of wrath to transform you into the children of adoption; from the state of guilt to accomplish such a mighty and a wonderful change upon you, as to put you into the state of justification; from the servants of sin to make you . . . the willing servants of God; to chase away from your faculties the darkness of nature, and to make all light and comfort around you . . . to pull down the strongholds of corruption within you, and raise him who was spiritually dead to a life of new obedience — this is the victory over you which God aspires after. . . .

It is your thorough and complete salvation from the punishment of sin, and the power of sin, on which He is desirous of exalting the glory of His strength, and this is the strength which He calls you to take hold upon.

If your child has not been wowed by grace, perhaps it's time to lead your child to preaching and preachers who thunder the wrath of God and gloriously proclaim the One who satisfies the wrath of God.

If you regularly show Jesus to be the most amazing pursuit anyone can dedicate their lives to, when sex, drugs, and rock-n-roll come calling, your child will respond by saying, "Are you kidding? Why would I settle for you when I have Christ?"

– Reset –

If the primary object of your child's affections is anything but Jesus, you have some work to do.

Chapter 11

Teach Your Children How the Bible Works

Imagine the Bible was written like a how-to manual, with page after page of rules for every single situation in every Christian's life for all time. Two major problems:

1. That would be one big book.
2. That would be one boring book.

Instead, our brilliant God gave us something more comprehensive and far more interesting. He gave us an action book filled with human stories that apply to every single situation in every Christian's life, forever. There is just one little catch; in order to read it right, children need to learn how to read it right.

Chances are pretty good that your kids think the Bible is filled with interesting, yet disjointed, tales. When we teach Bible stories as life lessons, the Bible becomes a morality book that is somewhat baffling and nonsensical.

Most kids raised in a Christian home know the story of Jesus, and Samson, and David, and Abraham, and Moses, and Solomon; but they don't understand the order, flow, or purpose of all of these historical accounts. To most kids, the Bible is a hodge-podge of cool stories with a fair amount of boring stuff. This is the child who quickly becomes untethered from a book that is clearly not special, let alone supernatural.

Because of that, most kids don't venture to pick up the Bible on their own, nor do they learn how to find the answers to life's pressing questions. We need to pre-empt and correct that confusion, or our children will never believe the Bible is sufficient for all of life and godliness (2 Timothy 3:16–17). We need to show our kids how the Bible works.

If our children don't learn how to stand on the reliable rock of God's Word, they will topple and fall when the world presses in. It happens all the time. So, let's take a look at how the Bible works (how it flows), and then we will take a look at how the Bible works (applies to our lives).

The Bible Is One Story

While there are many stories contained in the Bible, the Bible has only one theme: redemption. If we read random stories from the Bible, without teaching the singular theme of the Bible, our kids will not understand how elegant the Scriptures are. As you read through the Bible with your kids, watch for the rather bloody theme of redemption.

> **Story 1:** When Adam and Eve sinned in a perfect garden, God shed the first blood ever in order to cover the shame of two sinners (Genesis 3:21). Man's effort to cover their sin was not enough, God had to cover their sin with the shedding of blood.

> **Story 2:** Cain offered God a sacrifice from his crops: not acceptable. Abel offered God a blood sacrifice from his crops: acceptable (Genesis 4:4-5).

> **Story 3:** Abraham almost shed the blood of his only beloved son on a mountain located outside modern-day Jerusalem (Genesis 22:5–8). Two thousand years later, God actually sacrificed His only beloved Son on the same mountain (Isaiah 53:10).

> **Story 4:** If the exiled Jews would sacrifice a lamb and paint the blood on their doorposts, death would pass over His people (Exodus 12:2, 5–7, 12–13). Fifteen hundred years later, Jesus became the Passover lamb who shed His blood so death would pass over His church (1 Corinthians 5:7).

> **Story 5:** In about 1444 B.C., God initiated a lamb's blood sacrificial system for the Jewish people to have their sins covered (Leviticus 16). Fourteen centuries later, John the Baptist pointed to Jesus and announced, "Behold, the lamb of God who takes away the sin of the world" (John 1:29). Jesus was both the

sacrificial lamb who pays for our sins, and our scapegoat who removes our sins.

Story 6: Seven hundred years before Jesus was brutally beaten and slaughtered for the sins of others, Isaiah tells the story of a man who was brutally beaten and slaughtered for the sins of others (Isaiah 52:13–53:12).

Story 7: When Jesus ascended to heaven, having obtained eternal redemption by the shedding of His blood, He entered the holy place where He is currently mediating the new covenant (Hebrews 9:11–15).

Story 8: At a predetermined date in the future, Jesus will return to earth with blood on His thighs to pour out His wrath on the unredeemed and gather together His elect so they can dwell in a restored and perfect garden where the Lamb is the light (Revelation 21–22).

Knowing the redemptive theme of the entire Bible helps our kids understand how the Bible flows in an orderly fashion. As you highlight redemption throughout the Bible, you will be teaching your children the singular theme of the Bible. They will see it as a seamless book, not a confused hodge-podge of disjointed stories.

There is another way to help your child harmonize the Scriptures — teach them about biblical covenants. Understanding the major covenants is the key to understanding the flow of the Bible.

The Bible Is a Book of Covenants

When you placed a wedding ring on your spouse's finger and promised to be faithful "'til death do you part," you were participating in a covenant union. That is what a covenant is — a binding contract between two individuals 'til death do they part.

A biblical covenant is a life-long contract between two parties. At a covenant ceremony, the two parties read their vows and swear to not break their covenant vows, or suffer the consequence: death. A witness would write down the terms of the deal in a testament. That is why we have an Old and New Testament; it is the writing down of the terms of two covenants. That is why we sometimes call them the Old Covenant and the New Covenant, instead of Old Testament and New Testament.

In the Bible, we see several covenants between God and man, but there are three main covenants that, if rightly understood, will make the entire Bible make sense to your child.

The Abrahamic Covenant is God's promise to the first Jewish man that there would always be a land (Israel), a nation (the Jews), and a Seed (Jesus Christ). This was a one-sided covenant whereby God promised to always provide these three things (Genesis 15–22). This covenant is irrevocable.

The Mosaic Covenant is a two-person, mutually agreed upon covenant between God and the nation of Israel that promises blessings for obedience and curses for disobedience (Deuteronomy 28). If the Jews kept God's laws, God would bless them. If they were disobedient, God would curse them. This contract was a quid-pro-quo covenant.

The New Covenant is based on the redemptive work of the Seed, Jesus. This eternal covenant is the fulfillment of the Abrahamic Covenant, which cannot be broken. God alone wrote, orchestrated, and fulfills the promises of this new covenant. This new covenant abrogates the entire Mosaic covenant (Hebrews 8–10). With these three covenants in mind, let's fly through the Bible again and see if we can make sense of it for our kids.

God made two perfect people in the garden who sinned and deserved death. God immediately promised to provide a Savior who would bring life to people who deserve death (Genesis 3:15).

To accomplish His plan of redemption, God promised a man named Abraham that he would deliver on His promise by selecting a specific piece of property (Israel), inhabited by a special, chosen, holy nation (the Jews), which would ultimately produce a Seed (Jesus).

Abraham, the first Jew, had a grandson named Jacob who had 12 children. These children moved to Egypt to avoid starving to death by famine. Unfortunately, after the death of the pharaoh who was kind to the Jews, the new pharaoh wasn't keen on those interlopers, so he put them to work as slaves. They responded by having children, lots and lots of children.

God raised up a deliverer to move His chosen people into His Promised Land to live as a set-apart people who would produce a unique and special Seed. God gave Moses pages of laws to ensure His chosen people would be set apart from every other nation.

The rest of the Old Testament portrays the tug between the Abrahamic and Mosaic Covenants until God instituted the new and better covenant through Jesus, thus replacing the Old/Mosaic Covenant.

➢ Why did the Jews go into several captivities? Because they were suffering the consequences of violating the Mosaic Covenant.

➢ Why didn't God keep the Jews in exile? Because of the Abrahamic Covenant.

➢ Why is the Book of Esther in the Bible when it doesn't even reference God? Because this was a harrowing story of God's chosen people living under judgment of the Mosaic Covenant, being saved from extinction by a brave woman in fulfillment of the Abrahamic Covenant.

This is the Old Testament in a nutshell: God's chosen people, the Jews, lived in a promised land called Israel until God sent the promised Seed at just the right time to redeem for Himself a holy, set-apart people called the Church.

Plug the great stories of Moses, David, Habakkuk, and Zephaniah into that narrative, and these historical accounts will move from confusion to illumination as our kids watch God unfold His pre-arranged plan of redemption. Understanding these three covenants will help your child make sense of the Bible.

The Bible Is Progressive

If the Bible seems somewhat cryptic to your child, teach them that the Bible is a progressive revelation. God's story of redemption did not take place in an instant. God took centuries to accomplish His perfect plan, and we get to witness that plan gradually unfold.

> Concerning this salvation, the prophets, who spoke of the grace that was to come to you, searched intently and with the greatest care, *trying to find out the time* and circumstances to which the Spirit of Christ in them was *pointing* when he predicted the sufferings of the Messiah and the glories that would follow. It was revealed to them that they were not serving themselves but you, when they spoke of the things that *have now been told you* by those who have preached the gospel to you by the Holy Spirit sent from heaven. Even angels *long to look* into these things (1 Peter 1:10–12; NIV; emphasis added).

Even the angels didn't know how God was going to pull off the greatest story ever told. They had to wait and watch God advance His grand rescue story.

Every heroic movie and book is patterned after the cosmic reality of the greatest hero story ever told, which progressively unfolds like an epic movie that we get to watch when we read our Bibles.

History always requires time, and the history of Jesus took four thousand years to fully reveal. The Bible moves from fuzzy to clear. As we read through the Bible, we get more and more information about the character and nature of God as He delivers on His promise of a Deliverer.

Your child should not expect to know everything about God after reading Genesis 1:1. Your child will not understand everything about heaven, hell, sin, and redemption by reading the books of Moses. Let your child enjoy the progression of the Bible as they learn more and more about God as they go.

The Bible Is Not about Morals

If we overlook the grace of God as we read our Bibles, and simply point out proper Christian behavior, then Christianity becomes a mere morality tale of works, not grace. Instead, read the Bible to your children with gospel goggles on.

Don't read the story of the wee little man in the tree whom Jesus called down, and say, "When you have done something wrong, make sure you make things right, like Zacchaeus did" (Luke 19:8). Try this instead. "Look at how kind Jesus is! He saved a criminal who stole from poor people. That is precisely what He came to do, seek and save the lost, even criminals (Luke 19:10). If Jesus can save Zacchaues, He can save you." Then you can tell them that Zacchaues is a pristine example of the truly repentant heart described in 2 Corinthians 7:9–11.

The former places a heavy yoke on our kids. The latter helps our kids love the Lord and desire to make things right when we sin against someone.

The Bible Is Sufficient

After your child knows how the Bible works (how it flows), then you can teach them how the Bible works (how it applies to their lives). If you can demonstrate how the Bible can guide them through life, then they will turn first to Scriptures to find the answer to the questions they will inevitably ask:

> ➢ Who should I marry?
> ➢ Which car should I buy?

➤ Where should I go to college?

➤ Which house should I buy?

➤ What should I do for a living?

Countless kids torture themselves trying to figure out God's will for their lives, when God's will has already been revealed to them in the Bible. There is no need for your child to read tea leaves, throw out fleeces, or beg God to reveal the answer to their pleading prayers. All they need to do is read the Bible rightly to discover God's will for their lives.

The formula for decision-making is not necessarily easy, but it is quite simple.

1. Pray to God for wisdom, not the answer.
2. Read every verse in the Bible that speaks about your subject.
3. Seek godly, biblical wisdom from elders and loved ones who know you well.
4. Consider your preferences.
5. Make a decision.

When your child follows these steps and pulls the trigger, that is God's will for their life, even if it is a crummy decision. NOBODY does anything outside of God's providential will. We can do things outside of His revealed and moral wills, but we are never outside of what He ordains. God's will is revealed as we make decisions, good or bad.

God hides the future from us (Deuteronomy 29:29) and we should not petition Him to give us a sneak peek or drop hints from heaven. That is not how God operates. God gives us a Bible, godly counsel, a brain, and He let's us choose what we prefer as long as it is in alignment with His Word. That is extremely liberating.

Buying a Car

It is time for your son to buy his first car. Wanting to make the best choice, he prays, "O Lord, should I buy the super slick $40,000 orange sports car, or the practical and affordable $4000 blue Honda? Please reveal your will. Give me a sign."

He spends the next week looking for clues that might provide a glimpse into God's will for his life. Every time he sees a Honda he wonders, "Does God want me to buy the blue car?" While watching cable TV he stumbles across the Dukes of Hazard and sees the General Lee and thinks, "That's it! God must be telling me to buy the orange muscle car."

That is a horrible way to make decisions that have left many mumbling, "I made the wrong decision. Why didn't God give me clearer omens?" Instead, your child should:

1. Ask God for wisdom to make a car-purchasing decision that is wise, exhibits good stewardship, and will not compromise his Christian testimony.
2. Read every Bible verse about money, possessions, idolatry, and worldliness. He should also study Christian liberty: we might be permitted to buy something, but we give up that right if it compromises our testimony with other Christians or the world.
3. Ask parents and other elders for godly, biblical wisdom.
4. He can then consider if he likes the orange or blue car better.
5. He should think deeply about those four things and make a decision. Whichever automobile he chooses, that car is God's will for his life.

Now, let's say your son foolishly buys the pricey orange sports car that puts him in debt, drives up his insurance rates, and keeps him from attending college. That is still God's will for his life. Now your son can learn from the error that God permitted him to make. Ahhhh, what a relief.

Let's say your son wisely buys the reliable and affordable Honda. Then that was God's will for his life. How do I know? Because nothing happens outside of God's wills. That was not a typo. God has several wills:

➤ His perfect will revealed in the Bible.
➤ His permissive will that allows His creatures to make sinful decisions.
➤ His providential will: God's orchestrating and ordaining of every single human action for His glory.

Let's say your lead-foot son bought the orange car because:

➤ He wanted to look cool.
➤ He failed to understand stewardship.
➤ He didn't concern himself with his Christian testimony.

Then your child was outside of God's perfect will, but he was not outside God's providential will. If a child makes a sinful decision, it is ultimately good for the child because God only does good things for us, even if it hurts.

God does not ask us to be mystical sleuths who interpret signs in order to decide what we should do. God gives us prayer, His Word, wise counsel, and a brain, and we are to make decisions by utilizing all of those gifts.

We do not make decisions because we have a "peace about it." We make decisions because we have biblical wisdom. Teach your children to use the Bible to find answers to life's questions with the confidence that it has everything necessary for them to choose wisely and live rightly (2 Timothy 3:16–17).

If you teach your children how the Bible works, you will be doing them a profound favor. You will be setting their feet on a rock from which they will never slip.

– Reset –

If your child doesn't run to the Bible to make wise decisions, then you have some instructing to do.

Chapter 12

Don't Torque Your Kids

Considering the magnitude of the subject, it is rather shocking that the Bible says so little about parenting. There are basically two parenting verses in the entire Bible. Two! Here they are:

> These words, which I am commanding you today, shall be on your heart. You shall *teach them diligently* to your sons and shall talk of them when you sit in your house and when you walk by the way and when you lie down and when you rise up (Deuteronomy 6:6–7; emphasis added. There are other Old Testament verses, but they give the same instructions: Genesis 18:19; Deuteronomy 4:9, 11:19; Psalm 78:4).

> Fathers, do not *provoke your children to anger*, but bring them up in the discipline and *instruction of the Lord* (Ephesians 6:4; emphasis added).

There you go, Mom and Dad, two whole verses to equip you to successfully raise your children. And they are more than enough, even though they pretty much say the same thing.

We are to teach the Bible to our kids, and not make them angry. If we teach our kids the Bible while not making them bonkers, then we are doing everything God requires of us as parents. Unfortunately, it is very, very easy to neglect the one and excel at the other.

Permit me to step to the front of the line and confess. I have done plenty of things to exasperate my children. Here are the top ten ways I have made my kids angry:

Parenting Mistakes I Have Made

1. Didn't apologize enough. Oh, how often I have biffed it with my kids. Because of my self-righteousness, I regularly refused to humble myself and ask for their forgiveness. I must have made them angry countless times.

2. Did more faultfinding than praising. While the Bible doesn't list "faultfinding" as a spiritual gift, I have it in spades. If I could go back and do it all over again, I would praise them ten times for every critique.

3. Did not recognize their rotten fruit had not fallen far from the tree. I regularly exasperated them by being exasperated that they could be such little sinners. I forgot they inherited that propensity from me.

4. Did not ask for their preferences. Even adults have preferences; why can't kids? If only I had respected them when they said, "Dad, we don't like watching *Elvis, Aloha from Hawaii* every Friday night."

5. Didn't adjust my sense of humor for them. Sarcasm is biblical and it can be used affectively and even affectionately. But girls, as a rule, hate it. I failed to recognize that early and adjust accordingly. Every sarcastic remark (another spiritual gift) cut them to the quick and undoubtedly angered them.

6. Expected them to get over it when I wouldn't. "Just get over it," I barked, as I continued to harbor the very same grudge. How frustrating for them.

7. Forgot I am not a professional poker player. While I don't think I have ever yelled at my kids, I sure have shown them my mean face. Our faces are telling — they reflect what is happening in our hearts. How many times did I provoke them by giving them my trademarked angry/disappointed/disgusted face?

8. Expected their spiritual maturity to be the same as mine. Why did I regularly fail to remember that my children's spiritual maturity level shouldn't be the same as mine? If it were, I would be in big trouble.

9. I hurt feelings more than I realized. There are so many ways to frustrate our kids, and I think I have discovered all of them.

I have rolled my eyes at them. I have not shared with them. I have demoralized them by getting into the car with my licensed teenager and saying, "Are you kidding? I'll drive."

10. Separated the gospel from correction. When I barged into their rooms with the dreaded wooden spoon, they knew they weren't going to hear a Bible story.

Have you made these parenting mistakes? Join the club. Just make sure you also join the repentant club. Remember, these are not mere oopsies; these anger-inducing failures are sins. Repent to your God and to your children. Get the slate wiped clean. Heal. Move forward.

How to Spank

A number of years ago I was given a tour through St. Jude's Children's Research Hospital in Memphis. When I asked the doctors what was the hardest thing for the young patients with life-threatening illnesses, their answer was quite surprising. According to these doctors, the kids lamented that their parents never say no or spank them. That's right — these kids missed parental discipline. They intuitively knew that discipline demonstrates love. At least it should.

Too often we discipline in anger. Discipline should say, "I care for you." Furious parents who spank say, "I am irritated by you, and I don't care about you." Who can blame them for being angry when we spank them that way?

If you want to keep your kid from getting angry, resenting you, and hating God, here are some discipline thoughts.

1. Our goal is always the gospel. If we discipline without saturating our words with the gospel, then we are doing it wrong.
2. Remember, your children are image bearers of Almighty God. Handle with care.
3. Remember your role: you represent God to your children.
4. Differentiate between sins and preferences. A sin might require corporal punishment; a preference can be overlooked.
5. Determine wisely if their action was a sin, or just a mistake.
6. Don't accuse, ask. Nobody likes to have a finger poked in their chest.

7. Some fools need a rod; other fools need instruction. Determine which type of fool you are dealing with.

8. Explain the issue in biblical terms. Call their sin, sin. Then you can explain the reason for the spanking, and then you can take him/her to the Cross.

9. Don't be the sole prosecutor; help them examine themselves.

10. Talk to them, not at them or down to them.

11. Help them find the idol that is driving their behavior.

12. Discipline without biblical instruction and you will not be discipling your child.

13. Discipline privately. None of us likes to be undressed in front of others.

14. Remember that you cannot force heart-felt repentance.

15. If you are yelling, you are not parenting; you are sinning.

Corporal punishment is one of the kindest things we can do for our children. If we do it lovingly and biblically, then we are helping our children love God. When we do it wrongly, we are giving our kids a reason to hate God.

When we discipline our children with anything but the desire to help them love Jesus more, we fail them. And make them furious.

Take a moment to think through these questions. When you discipline your child:

➤ What is your tone?
➤ What is your volume?
➤ What does your face say?
➤ What does your heart say?
➤ Do you discipline to correct their behavior, or the state of their relationship with God?

If you are not sure, ask your spouse. If you really have courage, ask your children. If they respond by turning around and running away from you like the Road Runner, you have your answer.

Perhaps you naturally think your spouse and kids will praise you for being the best parent ever. Then kindly consider all of the ways we can exasperate our children. Here are 25 ways you can make your children fume. This list is courtesy of biblical counselor Lou Priolo.[1]

---

1. Lou Priolo, *The Heart of Anger* (Amityville, NY: Calvary Press, 1997).

1. Lack of marital harmony (they hate it more than you do)
2. Establishing and maintaining a child-centered home
3. Modeling sinful anger
4. Habitually disciplining in anger
5. Scolding
6. Being inconsistent with discipline
7. Having double standards
8. Being legalistic
9. Never admitting you're wrong
10. Constantly finding fault
11. Reversing God-given roles
12. Not listening to your child's opinion or taking his/her side of the story seriously
13. Comparing them to others unfavorably
14. Not making time "just to talk"
15. Not praising or encouraging your child
16. Failing to keep your promises
17. Chastening in front of others
18. Not allowing enough freedom
19. Allowing too much freedom
20. Mocking your children
21. Abusing them physically
22. Ridiculing or name-calling
23. Having unrealistic expectations
24. Practicing favoritism
25. Child training with worldly methodologies inconsistent with God's Word

Feel free to put this book down and get yourself some ice for those bruises. Oh, how many times I exasperated my children. I have a lot of repenting to do. How about you?

Let's not compound our failures by refusing to repent of these sins to our children. If we refuse to humble ourselves, then God will. Worse than that, we will be disobeying God's command to not make our kids angry. Unrepentant parents are infuriating. And angry kids don't typically grow up to be believing adults; they just get angrier.

– Reset –

If you have been making your children angry, you have not been helping them love Jesus.

Chapter 13

Act Like a Good Shepherd

L isten. Listen very carefully. If you turn your ear toward California or Missouri, you will hear the sound of millions of children getting enticed into a dangerous, sensual, and heretical movement. And there is a pretty good chance your kids are singing their songs.

Unfortunately, the fastest-growing Christian sect in the world is not Christian at all. The New Apostolic Reformation Movement boasts hundreds of millions of followers. The epi-centers of the NAR are located in Redding, California, and Kansas City, Missouri, but their reach is global.

The New Apostolic Reformation Movement barely teaches theology, and when it does, it is almost always wonky. Just one example will suffice.

Former Fuller Seminary professor and self-proclaimed prophet of the New Apostolic Reformation, C. Peter Wagner, preached that Japan's economy is struggling because the emperor had intercourse with the Sun Goddess. 'Nuff said.

Why are 369 million people attracted to this a-biblical form of Christianity?

1. They get attracted to the teachings of false prophets through the music of the mega-popular worship groups Jesus Culture and Hillsong. Kids love their hypnotic, romantic, and repetitious tunes. They hear the music at youth group and church, and assume the adults are okay with them. When they attend their concerts, they get introduced to the teachings of these aggressive recruiting machines.
2. Followers of the New Apostolic Movement love bomb emotionally starved college and high school students with hugs and kindness.

3. The teachings of the New Apostolic Movement are emotion-driven. It feels good, and millennials are hooked on that feeling.

4. The church services are very experiential. You don't think at an NAR worship service; you dance, jump, sway, get knocked down, and set on fire as the glory of God pours out of the ventilation system.

5. The NAR asks the kids to be a part of a great eschatological movement that ushers in the return of Jesus. These kids are told they could be a part of something big.

For a fuller treatment on the fastest-growing Christian sect in the world, I devoted two chapters to the NAR and Jesus Culture in my book, *Judge Not*. You can also see their histrionics on our DVD titled *Drunk in the Spirit*.

Mom and Dad, if you think this has nothing to do with you and your kids, ask them if they are familiar with Jesus Culture and Hillsong music. Ask them if they listen to their music. This cannot be stressed enough; music is the lure, but the false teachings of the NAR are the hook. And they are catching MILLIONS of kids.

Homes have been destroyed as families get torn apart. Parents' hearts have been shattered, and children's faiths have been shipwrecked. This aberrant movement is the single greatest external theological threat evangelicalism has ever seen. Do not dismiss this.

The NAR recruits with a ferocity that makes Mormons and Jehovah's Witnesses jealous. Your child will almost certainly be exposed to this movement and be invited to participate in a meeting, youth group, or concert that is NAR influenced. Are they prepared?

Jesus Understood the Consequences

It was none other than Jesus Christ who lobbed the first theological hand grenade that exploded all over the Pharisees. From John 5 through John 10, Jesus launched an intense theological assault against religious leaders. Jesus audaciously insisted that if they didn't know Him rightly, then they did not know the Father either (John 8:19). In other words, if you don't posses correct Christology, you will not be saved.

Jesus claimed to be God (John 8:58). Jesus claimed that He is the only means of salvation (John 14:6). Jesus claimed that if you don't understand His divine and human nature rightly, you will not be saved.

Jesus spent the entire fifth chapter of John testifying to the Pharisees that He is God. He equated Himself with the Father, over and over. Jesus knew they must understand that He and the Father are one or they would perish.

> He who *does not* honor the Son *does not* honor the Father who sent Him. Truly, truly, I say to you, he who hears *My word*, and believes Him who sent Me, has eternal life, and does not come into judgment, but has passed out of death into life (John 5:23–24; emphasis added).

If a child doesn't believe rightly in the One God sent, that child will perish eternally. In other words, correct Christology is kind of important.

> You *do not* have His word abiding in you, for you do not believe Him whom He sent (John 5:38; emphasis added).

Jesus went so far to say that a pastor who does not warn the flock about wolves are not true shepherds of Jesus Christ (John 10:12). Not that anyone else had to write about the subject after Jesus slammed the door shut on heresy, but the Apostles wrote extensively about the importance of correct theology.

The Apostle John Understood the Consequences

John closed his Gospel with his thesis statement for the book.

> Therefore many other signs Jesus also performed in the presence of the disciples, which are not written in this book; but these have been written so that you may *believe that Jesus is the Christ, the Son of God;* and that believing *you may have life* in His name (John 20:30–31; emphasis added).

John repeated this theme three times in his two epistles.

> Who is the liar but the one who denies that Jesus is the Christ? This is the antichrist, the one who *denies the Father and the Son.* Whoever denies the Son *does not* have the Father; the one who confesses the Son has the Father also (1 John 2:22–23; emphasis added).

> He who has the Son has the life; he who does not have the Son of God does not have the life (1 John 5:12).

> Anyone who goes too far and *does not* abide in the teaching of Christ, *does not* have God; the one who abides in the teaching, he has both the Father and the Son (2 John 9; emphasis added).

Apparently John thought theology was pretty important. Do your children?

Paul Understood the Consequences

Never one to pull his punches, Paul was anything but vague when it came to false teaching and false teachers. To the Judaizers in Galatia who were adding works (circumcision) to grace, he twice declared, "Let them be accursed" (Galatians 1:8–9). Paul even rebuked Peter publicly for confusing people about grace alone (Galatians 2:11–21).

Paul encouraged young Timothy to guard his doctrine closely (1 Timothy 4:16). Paul warned Timothy to reprove, rebuke, and exhort so his flock would not fall prey to false teachers (2 Timothy 4:2).

Paul's tearful farewell to the Ephesian elders summarizes Paul's ministry and concern for false teachings that can creep into a church.

> For I did not shrink from declaring to you the whole purpose of God. *Be on guard* for yourselves and for all the flock, among which the Holy Spirit has made you overseers, to shepherd the church of God, which He purchased with His own blood. I know that after my departure savage wolves will come in among you, not sparing the flock; and *from among your own selves* men will arise, speaking perverse things, to *draw away* the disciples after them. Therefore *be on the alert*, remembering that night and day for a period of three years I did not cease to *admonish* each one with tears (Acts 20:27–31; emphasis added).

Paul called false teachers savage wolves because he knew how dangerous they were. That is why Paul warned the Roman Christians to mark false teachers and avoid them (Romans 16:17).

If theology is no big whoop, then why are there so many warnings of false teachers in the Bible? Clearly, heresy is a big deal.

The Early Church Understood the Consequences

Heresy is a matter of eternal life or death. The early Church understood well the consequences of false beliefs: damnation. They took Jesus, John, Paul, Peter, and Jude seriously. When it came to theology proper, they understood the stakes were very high.

Do your kids know that the early Church fought prolonged battles with theological precision to make sure that everyone understood what must be believed if one is to be saved?

Consider Athanasius. This fourth century church father was exiled, jailed, and threatened for holding to orthodox Trinitarian theology. He stood *contra mundum* (against the world) to condemn the doctrine he knew would damn people who did not rightly understand the Trinity.

The creed that is named after him is a glimmering example of the concern the early Church had for incorrect Christology and correct Trinitarian theology. Here is about a third of the 43-sentence-long Athanasian Creed. It starts out with a kick: believe this statement of faith, or be damned. Not exactly seeker sensitive.

> Whosoever will be saved, before all things it is *necessary* that he hold the universal faith;
>
> Which faith except every one do keep whole and undefiled, without doubt he shall *perish everlastingly.*
>
> And the universal faith is this: That we worship one God in Trinity, and Trinity in Unity;
>
> Neither confounding the persons nor dividing the substance.
>
> For there is one person of the Father, another of the Son, and another of the Holy Spirit.
>
> As also there are not three uncreated nor three incomprehensible, but one uncreated and one incomprehensible.
>
> The Father is made of none, neither created nor begotten.
>
> The Son is of the Father alone; not made nor created, but begotten.
>
> The Holy Spirit is of the Father and of the Son; neither made, nor created, nor begotten, but proceeding.
>
> So there is one Father, not three Fathers; one Son, not three Sons; one Holy Spirit, not three Holy Spirits.

He therefore that will be saved must thus think of the Trinity.

Furthermore it is necessary to everlasting salvation that he also believe rightly the incarnation of our Lord Jesus Christ.

For the right faith is that we believe and confess that our Lord Jesus Christ, the Son of God, is God and man.

God of the substance of the Father, begotten before the worlds; and man of substance of His mother, born in the world.

Who, although He is God and man, yet He is not two, but one Christ.

This is the universal faith, which except a man believe faithfully he *cannot be saved* (emphasis added).[1]

Would your child be able to affirm that statement? Does your child comprehend the need for sound theology like the Council of Nicea, which literally fought over the Greek letter i?

The Council of Nicea contended that Jesus had the exact same nature as the Father (*homo-ousios*). They insisted that anyone who taught Jesus merely had a similar nature (*homoi-ousios*), would be damned. They literally fought over the letter i.

Do they know the Council of Chalcedon of A.D. 451 was dedicated to clarifying that Jesus had a fully divine and a fully human nature that never mixed or mingled? Here is the rather pithy Chalcedonian Creed. Prepare for the world's longest run-on sentence.

We, then, following the holy Fathers, all with one consent, teach men to confess one and the same Son, our Lord Jesus Christ, the same perfect in Godhead and also perfect in manhood; truly God and truly man, of a reasonable soul and body; consubstantial with us according to the manhood; in all things like unto us, without sin; begotten before all ages of the Father according to the Godhead, and in these latter days, for us and for our salvation, born of the virgin Mary, the mother of God, according to the manhood; one and the same Christ, Son, Lord, Only-begotten, to be acknowledged in two natures, inconfusedly, unchangeably, indivisibly, inseparably; the distinction of natures being by no means taken away by the union, but rather the property of each nature being preserved, and concurring in one Person and one

---

1. http://www.newadvent.org/cathen/02033b.htm.

Subsistence, not parted or divided into two persons, but one and the same Son, and only begotten, God the Word, the Lord Jesus Christ, as the prophets from the beginning have declared concerning him, and the Lord Jesus Christ himself taught us, and the Creed of the holy Fathers has handed down to us.[2]

Theological liberals, the NAR, and seeker-sensitive evangelicals scoff at such precision. We should not; eternity is at stake. The men who wrote our historic creeds were not knuckleheads.

Warn Them

The first thing we can do is warn our children that everyone who claims to be a Christian is not orthodox. Warn them of the wolves in apostle's clothing. Warn them that there are false teachers who would love their money, their bodies, and their souls.

Every book in the New Testament, but one, warns of false teachers. The entire Books of Jude and 2 Peter are dedicated to false teachers. Scripture is replete with commands to warn people about charlatans who masquerade as angels of light (2 Corinthians 11:14).

Teach Them Heresy

Don't indoctrinate your children with heresy, but teach them about historical heresies that just don't seem to go away. The Church has always had to battle heresy, and we are no different today.

Historically, there have been five basic heresies that continue to recycle throughout the centuries. These heresies reveal themselves in various forms.

The Judaizers

Paul's first-century battle was soteriological. The Judaizers of Galatia insisted that a man must be circumcised to go to heaven. Paul responded by condemning them the same way Jesus rebuked the Pharisees for adding works to grace.

The Gnostics

The big battle of the second century began a long history of Christological clashes. Gnosticism denied the incarnation of Jesus. They taught Jesus appeared to be a man, but was not actually a man (Docetism).

---

2. http://www.theopedia.com/chalcedonian-creed.

Arianism

Fast forward to the fourth century and another Christological lulu called Arianism. Arius denied the deity of Christ and the Trinity. Athanasius and the Council of Nicea disagreed and labeled Arianism a rank heresy.

The Pelagians

The fifth century brought us our last early Church soteriological battle. Pelagius denied total depravity and elevated free will above divine sovereignty in salvation. The early Church concluded: Pelagianism = heresy.

The Socinians

Rank heresy did not disappear entirely for 11 centuries, but it made a roaring comeback in the 16th century with the mother of all heresies. Laelius and Faustus Socinus took all of the aforementioned heresies, put all of these early Church heresies in a blender, and concocted a toxic mix . Socinianism is a legalistic, anti-Trinitarian, universalist, Christological, and soteriological mess that elevated reason above Scripture.

These five historical heresies are alive and well today. Mormons, Roman Catholics, liberal Protestants, Jehovah's Witnesses, Unitarians, Oneness Pentecostals, and many evangelicals have repackaged and re-pedaled these ancient heresies.

Warn your kids about these movements. Spend some time with them pointing out the bad currency, but spend even more time teaching them to identify the true currency.

Federal currency experts can spot a counterfeit from a mile away. Is it because they only study the knock-offs? No, they spend some time studying counterfeit currency, but they spend even more time studying the genuine article. The better they know the true, the easier it is to spot the false. The same thing is true with theology.

Immerse your children in the Bible and study the five solas of the Reformation. Teach them to know and love:

- ➤ *Sola Scriptura*: Scripture alone
- ➤ *Sola Gratia*: grace alone
- ➤ *Sola Fide*: through faith alone
- ➤ *Solus Christus*: through Christ alone
- ➤ *Soli Deo Gloria*: glory to God alone

The reformers drew very stark lines: anyone who fails to understand these five foundational truths stands outside of orthodoxy, and will be damned. If you don't want your kids to find their way into a wonky movement that will condemn their souls, warn them early and often that false beliefs are nothing to trifle with.

Make sure they grasp the doctrine of the Trinity. Make sure they possess correct Christology and soteriology. Make sure they understand the Bible is the inspired, infallible, inerrant, sufficient Word of God. After all, their souls depend upon it.

– Reset –

If you have withheld Jesus' warnings about heresy, you better get on it. Before it's too late.

Chapter 14

Don't Let Them Be Degraded or Shunned at Church

You would not want to stick around a church if you were treated like a toddler, publicly embarrassed, and chilled out by people who are supposed to love and care for you. And neither do our teenagers.

Based on my interaction with many kids who have jumped the Christian ship, they abandoned their parent's faith because they were degraded, disliked, and not respected in church. Who can blame them for not wanting to be a part of a church that does that?

Here are two scenarios that have caused too many kids to wave goodbye to the evangelical church.

Silliness

Attending most youth groups is not unlike attending a Gallagher concert. They are loud, messy, juvenile, not hip, and not very theological. The seeker-sensitive definition of a successful youth group is: FUN! Unfortunately, their definition of fun is: infantile nonsense.

Recently, two friends from two different churches sent me an email on the same day. Both emails contained a picture of an all too common scene. The first picture showed a 14-year-old boy with Life Savers® stuck to his face. He was the "winner" of his youth group's "suck on a Life Saver® and stick it to someone's face" competition. The person with the most sucked on Life Savers® stuck to his mug wins.

The second picture was a church Facebook photo of a different young boy who looked like he was chomping on something with his front teeth.

The thing he was chewing on was another boy's toenail. He won $20. It only cost him his dignity and reputation.

These two examples are the tip of the youth group iceberg that has shipwrecked the faith of many kids they think they are helping. So-called "Gross Out Games" are the norm in too many evangelical youth groups. They range from girls feeding Doritos® to boys with their bare feet, to drinking a can of soda through somebody else's dirty sock. If only I were making this up.

In an effort to be fun, these ubiquitous youth groups are downright degrading. Young adults are treated like children. No, scratch that, children shouldn't be treated so horrifically.

➤ Pressuring a boy to dress up like a girl, even in our progressive society, can only lead to taunting and abuse.
➤ Making boys wrestle girls in a kiddie pool filled with whipped cream can only lead to lust and sin.
➤ Making students lick peanut butter out of other student's toes can only lead to athlete's mouth.

This is not a joke. These shenanigans are going on in youth groups all across America; maybe in your church.

If a public school teacher treated children this way, the community would be outraged, and the teacher would be fired. In Evangelical churches, the pastor of toenail boy actually "liked" the Facebook photo.

Brandon

Let's follow the trajectory of "Brandon." Brandon can't remember not going to church with his parents. When Brandon becomes a teenager, he starts attending junior high youth group. Here, Brandon is introduced to ice-breakers like "Alka-Seltzer® on the Head Duel." The next week he competes in "Baby Bottle Burp" dressed in a bib and fed baby food by a female student who then burps him like a baby.

Throughout junior high he wins an occasional round of "Banana Barf," but senior high youth group introduces him to a whole new level of ridiculous. While he enjoys the ice cream as he plays "Banana Split Feet," lustful thoughts fill his brain as a female student makes the banana split and feeds it to him with her bare feet.

At least he wasn't chosen for "Jello Twister," "Porridge Pants," or "Wrestling in Cream Corn." He did, however get goaded into playing "Beautiful Boys." He looked quite pretty after a girl put makeup, earrings, jewelry, and hair clips on him while the youth pastor applauded.

Upon graduating from high school, Brandon leaves for college and finds himself rooming with a Roman Catholic. He learns that his Catholic buddy was never made to drink a Coke through another student's stinky sock. Brandon starts attending his roommate's Catholic campus church.

Brandon's mom and dad are shocked when their son informs them he has converted to Roman Catholicism. Can you blame him? Brandon had been degraded (and in my opinion, abused) for years in his evangelical youth group, which rarely even talked about God.

Even Worse

While this may be hard to believe, there is something even worse than the gross-out games many evangelical youth groups play: the abysmal effort to make Christian teaching cool. Youth ministers just don't think theology can hold the attention of electronically addicted teens, so they try to put some razzle-dazzle into their watered down, moralistic teaching.

How bad is it? I only had to visit one youth group website to discover the ridiculous, but true, gross out games listed above. Most of the games described at these sites, didn't even explain the purpose of humiliating the children. Here is a description of one game that actually had an accompanying lesson.

Cake Head

This game is played up front with a few people while the crowd watches. Mix a cake on the head — yes, directly on the head — of a brave volunteer who will be a good sport if their hair gets messed up. Just dump it all on their head. Use cake mix, eggs, water, oil, and icing. Mmm, yummy. Lathers up good, too!

The Point

This can also be used as an illustration for a talk about faith and deeds. Without Christ as the foundation of a life, we can have all the righteous ingredients in our lives (church, Bible study, Christian friends, etc.), but they won't matter. If we don't have the right foundation, all that great stuff is useless.

Who needs the Bible when you can teach a lesson based on a puerile game? Instead of teaching our kids to build their lives on Jesus (Matthew 7:24–27), this youth pastor humiliates a student by putting cake mix on his head. Not exactly analogous; and yet this is all too common.

Caitlin

Meet Caitlin, who suffered the same youth group fate as Brandon. Upon arriving at college, she realizes she doesn't get relegated to the kids' table; instead the professors actually treat her with respect. They don't patronize, humiliate, or talk down to Caitlin. Caitlin admires these grown-ups who seem to be very erudite and caring. She compares these professors to her trendy eyeglass-wearing youth pastor, and Caitlin becomes fruit that is ripe for the secular humanist picking. As Caitlin grows in her admiration for the adults who don't treat her like a juvenile, she becomes increasingly open to their worldview. It doesn't take long for Caitlin to embrace evolution and the hook-up culture.

We should not be shocked or angry with Brandon and Caitlin. They are responding quite naturally to the ignominy they were exposed to in their childhood youth groups.[1]

Coldness

There is another scenario that causes kids to abandon their childhood faith. When children become young adults and feel a chill from their local church, they run as fast as they can to circles that will love and embrace them.

Most evangelical churches do a pretty stellar job of loving the little tykes, but as the children become adults, they seem to forget that these young adults actually notice if they are being ignored or talked down to.

As the teenager tries to integrate himself into the adult church world, he is frequently greeted with indifference. The big people give their attention to other big people, but have a tendency to ignore young adults.

Trevor

Trevor stands dutifully next to his parents while they chitchat in the lobby of the church. None of the big people make eye contact with Trevor. The adults are pleasant with his parents, but they totally ignore him. Their shunning actually feels worse than being spurned by the cool clique in his

---

1. http://www.thesource4ym.com/games/default.aspx?Search=Sick.

youth group. Trevor concludes that church people are phony: they are nice to some people, but not nice to everyone.

In the mini-van on the way home, Mom asks Trevor why he's so quiet. "I'm fine," he mutters. The family heads to IHOP®, but Trevor is feeling unwelcomed and unloved. What's worse is that he doesn't think his parents would even understand.

When Trevor gets to his university, his fraternity welcomes him with open arms. They like him and include him in events. They help him with homework. He feels loved.

On the night of the frat party, Trevor's newfound friends chant, "Chug, chug, chug." Trevor happily participates to make his newfound friends think he's cool. He does not want to lose their affection.

Madison

Madison is even more perceptive than Trevor. She sees how the old people look at her when she dares to wear something hip to church. She feels their gazes piercing right through her. She concludes they are disgusted with her. That suspicion is confirmed when an adult disparagingly says, "You have two ear piercings. Do your parents know about this?"

When an adult asks Madison what college she plans to attend, her response is greeted with an incredulous, "Why in the world would you want to go there?" Madison is feeling something, but it isn't love.

When Madison gets to her university, she is lost, uncertain, and a bit dazed. As she walks to the student center, a very nice group of sophomores, who appear to be having a great time, approach her and ask, "Would you like a hug? You look like you need a hug."

The next week, Madison begins attending the student New Apostolic Reformation meeting with her new friends who love her. She has been love bombed, and she happily succumbs.

Loving Our Kids

George Barna hasn't done a poll on this yet, but I think the following formula, while not perfect, is reliable.

> Liberal churches = warmer people.
> Conservative churches = colder people.

Permit me to say this as a conservative Christian; we can indeed be the frozen chosen.

> ➤ Is it because unloving people are attracted to conservative theology and loving people gravitate toward liberalism? I don't know.
> ➤ Is it because head knowledge that doesn't make it to the heart makes people crabby? I don't know.
> ➤ Is it because liberals tend to focus on helping others while conservatives focus on internal sanctification? I don't know.

Visit a Charismatic church and I guarantee you will be welcomed with literal open arms. You will feel the love. You don't get that sort of welcome at most conservative churches.

If our churches do not love and respect our young adults, then they will find a church, lover, or substance that will love them. That includes your children.

Think about your church for a moment. Has your church been honoring your teenagers, or degrading them by peer pressuring them to participate in gross-out games? Does your teenager feel welcomed and loved by the adults at church? Does your child feel shunned, respected, or degraded?

Now, think about your home. Do you respect your child? Do you talk down to your child? Do you show interest in your child? Do you show affection to your child? If you don't, chances are very good, someone else will.

– Reset –

If we do not respect and love our children, we should not be surprised if they seek love and respect elsewhere.

Chapter 15

Answer the Big "Why" Questions

Who am I, why am I here, and where am I going when I die? Every child eventually wants to know the answer to the great philosophical questions of life. Few find the answer, and the consequences of an untethered life are devastating.

➢ Being obedient is worthless.
➢ Doing schoolwork is pointless.
➢ Getting married is purposeless.
➢ Having children is meaningless.

It is our great privilege to inform our children that God does indeed have a wonderful plan for their lives. Not in a seeker sensitive kind of way, but in a far more grand and profound way.

If you can biblically instruct your children to understand the big questions of life, you will be preparing them to live a life of contentment and hope. If you do not, a child will live his life like a pagan: pointless and despairing.

Who Am I?

Talk about a privilege! We get the joy of telling our kids:

➢ They are not lucky primordial ooze.
➢ God thought of them before eternity began (Ephesians 1:4).
➢ They are fearfully and wonderfully made by God Himself (Psalm 139:14).

> ➤ They are designed to resemble God Himself (Genesis 1:26).

> ➤ They are higher, better, and smarter than animals (Genesis 1:26).

The world tells us that everyone is special because of their skills or contributions to society (utilitarianism). The Bible tells us we are special because we are individually designed by God and for God. This knowledge does not inflate pride; it develops a profound humility as we consider that God actually thought of us gazillions of years ago.

Knowing that we are each intricately designed by God Himself (Psalm 139:13–16) gives us dignity, humility, purpose, and hope. It also increases our love for God when we consider that He thought of us before the foundation of the world, and He actually carried out His plans and made us.

Schools tell our children they are no better than a sea slug. We need to be telling our children they are the exclusive image bearers of Almighty God. That is the kind of knowledge that beckons a child to run to God, not from Him.

Why Am I Here?

The purpose of man is simultaneously simple and unimaginably amazing. Ten verses in Ephesians 2 answers the teleological whopper, "Why am I here?"

> And you were *dead* in your trespasses and sins, in which you formerly walked according to the course of this world, according to the prince of the power of the air, of the spirit that is now working in the *sons of disobedience*. Among them *we too* all formerly lived in the lusts of our flesh, indulging the desires of the flesh and of the mind, and were by nature *children of wrath*, even as the rest (Ephesians 2:1–3; emphasis added).

Those verses aren't exactly a recipe for healthy self-esteem; we are dead in our trespasses and sin. We are sons of disobedience, and God's wrath abides upon us. Thankfully, Ephesians 2 continues with one of the best words in the Bible, "but."

> *But* God, being rich in *mercy*, because of His great *love* with which He loved us, even when we were dead in our transgressions,

> *made us alive* together with Christ (by grace you have been saved), and *raised us up* with Him, and *seated us* with Him in the heavenly places in Christ Jesus (Ephesians 2:4–6; emphasis added).

Because God is merciful and loving, He rescues us, redeems us, and He is going to resurrect us. We get to live with Him. We get to reign with Him. We get to be served by Him. Why has God done such wonderful things?

> *So that* in the ages to come He might show the surpassing riches of His *grace* in *kindness* toward us in Christ Jesus. For by grace you have been saved through faith; and that not of yourselves, it is the gift of God; not as a result of works, so that no one may boast (Ephesians 2:7–9; emphasis added).

Philosophers can stop philosophizing; the mystery has been solved. The purpose of man's existence is to bring great glory to God by getting saved. God's Church has been chosen by Him to bring Him glory as He saves fallen image bearers by grace alone through faith alone in Jesus Christ alone. Now that is a wonderful plan for our lives.

When our kids understand that God is the star of this cosmic show in which we get to play a bit part, then, and only then, does life have meaning. Knowing that we were made to be saved by God makes the rest of life mere window dressing. Saved sinners spend our days bringing Him glory as we perform the tasks that He Himself has assigned us.

> For we are His workmanship, created in Christ Jesus for *good works*, which God prepared beforehand so that we would walk in them (Ephesians 2:10; emphasis added).

What your child does for a living is almost irrelevant in light of the bigger picture. We are not here to be doctors, lawyers, and street sweepers. We are here to glorify God by getting saved, and then doing the works that God has given us to do, whatever they are. Our identity is not defined by our business cards. Everyone's vocation is exactly the same: get saved and do what God has assigned you to do.

Martin Luther said the milkmaid serves God and loves her neighbor by providing milk for God's children to drink. Your child should see life that way.

➤ The lawyer serves God by rendering justice for fallen image bearers.
➤ The doctor serves God by healing sick image bearers.
➤ The street sweeper serves God by making transportation safe for commuting image bearers.
➤ The stay-at-home mom serves God by nurturing and instructing God's little image bearers.

Life is not about work; life is about serving God as we work, play, eat, drink, or whatever we do (1 Corinthians 10:31). The knowledge that we are not laborers, but God glorifiers, allows the Christian to do his job, as humdrum as it may be, with gusto. We can put our hearts and backs into mundane tasks, knowing that we are serving God by serving His image bearers.

> Were you called while a slave? Do not worry about it; but if you are able also to become free, rather *do that*. For he who was called in the Lord while a slave, is the *Lord's freedman*; likewise he who was called while free, is *Christ's slave*. You were bought with a price; do not become slaves of men (1 Corinthians 7:21–23; emphasis added).

What greater motivation to work than knowing that your boss is the God who died for you? That is better than a year-end bonus.

➤ Can a Christian desire a different career? Certainly, but as he waits, he can jump out of bed in the morning knowing that he isn't his job; he is a servant of the King of kings.
➤ Can a Christian desire to live in a different house in a different zip code? Absolutely, but until God provides that, we can be content knowing we are exactly where God wants us for as long as He chooses.
➤ Can a child desire to attend an Ivy League school? Sure, but if God doesn't provide the means for that to happen, then your child can be content knowing God wants him or her at a community college.

We have peace in trying situations because our biggest worry has been removed. You and I were on a highway to hell when God injected Himself and made Himself known to us (Ephesians 1:9). Because of Him, we have every spiritual blessing in the heavenly realm (Ephesians 1:3), specifically, the forgiveness of our sins (Ephesians 1:7).

When your children grasp that God freely offers His kingdom to wretched sinners, they will have humility and joy. And they will not come running when evolution calls them back to the swamp.

Where Am I Going?

Let's say your child ends up on a plane with Tom Hanks and winds up stranded on a deserted island without a Bible. Will they be able to say, "If I die, I will go to hell if I don't have my sins forgiven by Jesus Christ. But Mom and Dad always said I don't have to go to hell. They told me it is never too late to be saved if I repent and trust in Jesus"?

You don't want your child to end up on an island with a volleyball, not knowing how to find eternal life. I encourage you to so thoroughly indoctrinate your child in the glorious gospel that they accept it or reject it, but never forget it.

Your Child Is a Vessel

There are two types of human vessels: vessels fit for honor and vessels fit for dishonor.

> Now in a large house there are not only gold and silver vessels, but also vessels of wood and of earthenware, and *some to honor and some to dishonor* (2 Timothy 2:20; emphasis added).

Who exactly becomes a vessel of honor used by God for noble things?

> Therefore, if anyone *cleanses himself* from these things, he will be a vessel for honor, sanctified, *useful to the Master*, prepared for every *good work* (2 Timothy 2:21; emphasis added).

Would you like your child to be a vessel of honor used by the Lord for lofty things? Of course you would. Do you want your progeny to be a vessel of dishonor that is not useful for the Master? Of course not.

Then permit me to encourage you to give yourself a time-out and think long and hard about the orientation of your parenting. Does your child understand the answers to the questions of life they are sure to ask? If you do not tell them, someone else will.

– Reset –

If your children do not know the answers to life's biggest questions, you now have something to talk about at dinner tonight.

Chapter 16

Enroll Them in Ancestry.com/ Protestantism

There is a reason that Ancestry.com has over two million members; people love to know their heritage. Humans seem to have an innate desire to know where they came from. Your kids are no different.

There is a noteworthy trend that indicates young Protestants are swimming the Tiber to Roman Catholicism because they just don't think they have a heritage. While only two percent of evangelicals convert to Catholicism,[1] this is a trend that is growing and worth understanding. Two percent might not seem high, but that number is huge when it is your child.

With 81 million evangelicals in America,[2] two percent is a loss of over 1.6 million evangelicals to Rome. There are many reasons for this defection:

1. Evangelicals do not understand, and love being saved by grace alone.

2. The human propensity is to work for one's salvation. Roman Catholicism provides that opportunity.

3. Some evangelicals long for a more structured authority system. Rome definitely has that over Evangelicals (perhaps with the exception of Presbyterians, Anglicans, and confessional Lutherans).

4. Some Evangelicals long for a more intellectual approach to the faith. Catholics tend to write in a drier, more formal way, thus giving the impression their faith is smarter than the

---

1. http://fivethirtyeight.com/datalab/evangelical-protestants-are-the-biggest-winners-when-people-change-faiths/.

2. http://www.pewforum.org/2015/05/12/americas-changing-religious-landscape/.

Evangelical faith. Apparently these converts to Catholicism never discovered the Puritans.

5. Some people just like pomp and circumstance, a Roman Catholic specialty.

6. Catholic proselytes long for a system that has ancestry. They are told the Catholic Church has been around for two thousand years.

These Evangelicals flee to Rome because they are looking for a deeper connection, a heritage. They want to feel like they are a part of something big and old. They mistakenly think their Evangelical ancestry only goes back to Billy Graham (with the exception of a few Baptists who believe their denomination goes back to John the Baptist).

How do we correct this confusion? Simple: take them on a raucous ride through history by teaching them their Protestant heritage. These stories will capture their attention, and hold it as they hear about murder plots, kidnappings, narrow escapes, power struggles, slave ships, crying queens, wars, and torturous deaths. Best of all, they will meet their brilliant and brave spiritual relatives.

Take them back in time and introduce them to their Protestant ancestors who have been preaching the gospel of grace-alone for centuries. They will know that they are part of something old and big, and they won't be tempted when the pope calls.

John Wycliffe

John Wycliffe was the Morningstar of the Reformation. Wycliffe was the first priest to recognize the unbiblical errors that had crept into the Catholic Church since the sixth century. Contrary to the Catholic Church, Wycliffe preached:

➢ Justification is by grace alone.
➢ Jesus, not the pope, is the head of the church.
➢ Indulgences are unbiblical and contrary to grace.
➢ Works are a result of justification, not a part of it.
➢ The Bible alone is the church's sole source of authority.
➢ Communion bread and wine do not become the body and blood of Jesus.

For his trouble, Wycliffe lived and died in seclusion in 1384. The Catholic Church was so furious at Wycliffe that they declared him a heretic at the Council of Constance on May 4, 1415. His books were destroyed and his body was exhumed in 1428. Pope Martin V had his bones burned and his ashes tossed into the Swift River.

The chronicler Fuller observed:

> They burnt his bones to ashes and cast them into the Swift, a neighboring brook running hard by. Thus the brook hath conveyed his ashes into Avon; Avon into Severn; Severn into the narrow seas; and they into the main ocean. And thus the ashes of Wycliffe are the emblem of his doctrine which now is dispersed the world over.[3]

John Wycliffe is your child's spiritual ancestor. Have your children met him yet?

Jan Huss

Jan (John) Huss was a Bohemian priest who joined Wycliffe in his critiques of the Catholic Church. On the back wall of his church were two murals. One was a picture of the bejeweled pope riding a white stallion while people kissed his ornate rings. The other image was of Jesus entering Jerusalem on a donkey.

Huss (which means "goose") was told that the church wanted to have a little chat about some of his teachings. They lied. He was arrested and put in a foul dungeon near putrid plumbing for eight months. Huss was publicly mocked and excommunicated four times. Before being burned at the stake in 1415, Huss said,

> I would not for a chapel of gold, recede from the truth.
>
> I have never thought nor preached except with one intention of winning men, if possible, from their sins. Today, I will gladly die.

Foxe's *Book of Martyrs* provides the less than pleasant details.

> The flames were now applied to the sticks, when our martyr sung a hymn with so loud and cheerful a voice that he was

---

3. http://www.christianity.com/church/church-history/timeline/1201-1500/john-wycliffe-reformation-morningstar-11629869.html.

heard through all the cracklings of the combustibles and the noise of the multitude. At length his voice was interrupted by the severity of the flames, which soon closed his existence.

According to Kali Vota, the president of the Jan Huss society, Huss had his goose cooked for at least 15 minutes before the flames mercifully consumed him. This brave man is your child's great, great, great, great, great grandfather.

Jerome Savanarola

Jerome Savanarola was an Italian priest who railed against the corruption and debauchery he observed in the Roman Catholic Church.

> It is now time to open the den, we will turn the key, such a stench and so much filth will be vomited forth by Rome as will overspread all Christendom and everybody will be tainted by it.[4]

While Savanarola was less of a theological reformer and more of a moral reformer, he did teach justification by faith alone and the centrality of Scripture. The Church responded to their annoying priest by torturing Savanarola for weeks before hanging and burning him in 1498.

Charles Spurgeon preached this about Savanarola:

> "His Holiness" granted permission for the monk to be tortured. A recantation was demanded of him, but he refused. He was then stretched seven times during the week upon the rack. In the height of his sufferings he cried, "Lord, take my spirit," and, worn out by the tortures, he agreed to confess.
>
> When, however, he had rested a while, he withdrew his recantation, and boldly avowed all that he had previously taught.
>
> Between the day of his trial and the day of his execution he wrote an exposition of the fifty-first Psalm:
>
> "Alas wretch that I am, destitute of all help, who have offended heaven and earth — where shall I go? Whither shall I turn myself? To whom shall I fly? Who will take pity on me? To heaven I dare not lift up my eyes, for I have deeply sinned against it; on earth I find no refuge, for I have been an offence

---

4. Jerome Savanarola, *The Triumph of the Cross*, quoted at http://www.spurgeon.org/s_and_t/ tfm1869.php.

to it. What therefore shall I do? Shall I despair? Far from it. God is merciful, my Savior is loving. God alone therefore is my refuge."

Prior to being burned to ashes, the bishop deprived Savanarola of his priestly garments, saying, "Thus I exclude thee from the militant and triumphant church."

"From the church militant thou mayest," exclaimed Savanarola, "but from the church triumphant thou canst not." He died blessing the people who deserted him, and clinging to Christ whose love had never departed from him.[5]

Has your child met this distant Italian relative yet?

William Tyndale

William Tyndale was an English Roman Catholic priest of the 16th century who longed to see the Bible translated into the vernacular of the people. As the Latin Vulgate was the authorized Bible of the Catholic Church, Tyndale's plan was considered a big no-no. Tyndale fled Catholic persecution by hiding in Europe before being betrayed by a "friend."

Tyndale spent 18 months in a dark and dank prison in Vilvorde, Belgium. While languishing in jail, Tyndale continued to translate the Greek and Hebrew manuscripts of the Bible into English. He refused to recant for his Protestant beliefs and was strangled to death by a chain before his body was burned on October 6, 1536.

Foxe's *Book of Martyrs* paints a chilling picture.

> Then he was bound to the beam, and both an iron chain and a rope were put around his neck. Gunpowder was added to the brush and logs. At the signal of a local official, the executioner, standing behind Tyndale, quickly tightened the noose, strangling him. Then an official took up a lighted torch and handed it to the executioner, who set the wood ablaze.[6]

They strangled Tyndale so he couldn't preach justification by faith alone, the priesthood of all believers, that Jesus is the head of the Church, and denounce purgatory and praying to saints, before the flames silenced him.

---

5. Ibid.
6. http://www.christianitytoday.com/history/people/scholarsandscientists/william-tyndale.html.

William Tyndale was strangled and burned because he wanted your children to be able to read the Bible in English. Do they know that?

Martin Luther

Dr. Martin Luther spent his life on the run from a pope who desired to condemn and kill him for preaching justification by faith alone. He also wasn't nuts about how Luther talked about the office of the papacy, praying to saints, indulgences, and transubstantiation.

Luther risked his life so your child could be saved by grace alone. Do your children know that Protestant Martin Luther radically altered the history of the West?

Ulrich Zwingli

Ulrich Zwingli of Zurich, Switzerland, was a reformer who literally went to war in 1531 when Rome attacked his Swiss Protestant district. He was injured in battle and refused to give a confession to a Catholic priest on the field. For Tyndale's refusal to have his sins absolved by a mere mortal, they skewered him with a sword before quartering and burning him. Your child's last name probably isn't Zwingli, but your child is related to him nonetheless.

John Calvin

John Calvin was busy teaching Protestant theology in Geneva, Switzerland, in the 16th century, when the licentious Libertines brought charges against him. Calvin unbuttoned his shirt like Fabio, declaring, "If you want blood, there are still a few drops here. Strike then!" Calvin had no takers, but the Libertines would regularly fire their guns at Calvin's home and set their dogs on him when he was out of his house.

The Libertine conflict came to a head inside of Calvin's church. After preaching a sermon, Calvin quoted John Chrysostom, "I will lay down my life before these hands give the sacred things of God to those who have been branded as despisers."[7] Calvin would soon put his body where his mouth was.

A group of Libertines barged into Calvin's church and surrounded the Lord's Table. They threatened, "Administer communion to us or you will die." Calvin spread his arms over the elements, telling them they could cut

---

7. http://www.thirdmill.org/files/english/html/ch/CH.Arnold.RMT.9.HTML.

off his arms and spill his blood, but they could never force him to dishonor God by profaning the Lord's Supper. The Libertines left. The congregation took communion in silence.[8]

Despite being the skinniest man in Geneva, Calvin was willing to die so that your child could rightly celebrate the Lord's Supper.

Your Child's Heritage

You could go on and on with the harrowing tales of the hundreds of Protestants who were burned at the stake, courtesy of England's Bloody Mary. Or you could tell your kids that John Knox prayed and Queen Mary quaked, "I fear the prayers of John Knox more than all the assembled armies of Europe."[9]

Read Foxe's *Book of Martyrs* and dramatically show your kids their blood-stained heritage. Warn them to not run to Rome and deny all of the Protestant doctrines for which our ancestors gave their lives. The child who knows his/her Protestant heritage is more likely to remain Protestant.

– Reset –

If you don't want your child to swim the Tiber, teach them their Protestant Reformation heritage.

---

8. Ibid.
9. http://www.ligonier.org/learn/articles/give-me-scotland-or-i-die/.

Chapter 17

Put Armor on Your Children

Walk into virtually any church nursery in the West and you are likely to see a mural of Noah's cute little boat bobbing on the water, as a giraffe sticks his head out the window and smiles. Adorable? Yes. Helpful? Not so much.

When we portray biblical events as cartoon characters (or even worse, as vegetables), we encourage our children to think these stories are akin to a Hanna Barbera production. When they discover the "science of Darwin," they regularly jettison their childhood bedtime stories for "real knowledge."

The story of Noah's ark is not a fairy story. It is an accurate historical account of God's almost total annihilation of the world. It also explains why we see:

> ➤ Rapid or no erosion between strata
> ➤ The rapid burial of plants and animals
> ➤ Many strata laid down in rapid succession
> ➤ Sediment that has been transported long distances
> ➤ Fossils of sea creatures located high above sea level
> ➤ Rapidly deposited sediment layers spread across vast areas

Has your child been taught that the effects of the Flood are visually observable today? Has anyone in your church ever taught the global flood as the historical event that explains so much of our world?

Adam and Eve

Right next to the mural of Noah's cute little pets going for a boat ride is the image of the first two scantily clad humans, Adam and Eve. There they are, sharply dressed in fig leaves while taking a nosh out of a Honey Crisp Apple. While that may be intriguing to some children, it sure doesn't look like actual history to most children.

Christian children are inadvertently led to believe that schools teach facts, while the church teaches morality tales. Should we really be surprised when our youth get hammered by Darwinian evolution and fall like the stock market on Black Monday?

Once upon a time, the man assigned to read the Bible during the Sunday service would announce at the volume of 11, "Prepare now to hear the Word of God." The congregation understood they were not about to hear Aesop's *Tales*.

You and I need to declare the same thing to our kids when we read the Bible to them. They need to hear and feel that the Bible is the accurate, historical, and exclusive Word of God. Kids should sit up straight when they approach the reading of God's holy Word.

May I ask you some questions?

➤ Do you teach them to honor the Word of God?
➤ Do you read the Bible to your children as if God Himself wrote it?
➤ Do you teach the Bible to your children like it is the infallible, inerrant revelation of God to man?
➤ Do your children know that the Bible is not a storybook filled with tall tales of strong men and prophets who spend a three-day weekend in the belly of a big fish?

How you teach and read the Bible to your children will prepare them for the secular onslaught they will inevitably experience. Ignore this and you can look forward to your child slip sliding away.

Science or Fiction?

We need to instruct our kids about the "science of Genesis." While nobody alive today was an eyewitness to ancient historical events, we have an account from someone who was.

You do not need to become a scientist, but you can tap into the wealth of knowledge of very fine Christian scientists (not the Mary Baker Eddy kind). Answers in Genesis has done a very fine job of defending the historicity of the Book of Genesis. There are several reasons we should make an effort to educate our children about the importance and reliability of this foundational book:

> ➤ Genesis explains man's origins.
> ➤ Genesis explains why there is evil in the world.
> ➤ Genesis explains why humans are more valued to God than animals.
> ➤ Genesis explains where and how the institution of marriage originated.
> ➤ Genesis explains why the death penalty is the correct response to murder.
> ➤ Genesis explains why the Jewish people still exist and live in the land of Israel.
> ➤ Genesis explains why we have nations, borders, different languages, and different skin colors.
> ➤ Genesis refutes purposeless evolution, and forcefully declares that God created the world recently in six 24-hour days.

Teaching your kids the total reliability and historically accurate book called Genesis will prepare them to defend their biblical worldview when a professor pontificates, "Darwinian evolution gives us an intellectual reason to deny the existence of God."

Postmodernism

Your children are living in a postmodern world, and you do not want them to become a postmodern girl or boy. This recycled worldview has to be one of the devil's better strategies to lead our youth astray.

Postmodernism can be defined with one simple phrase, "Who am I to judge?" That is why the unbeliever's favorite misquoted Bible verse is, "Judge not." While postmodernism has existed before in the ancient world (think pluralistic Greece and Rome, or the time of the Judges), this recent incarnation has led countless Christian kids to question and abandon the faith.

Postmodernism is thoroughly secular. In fact, postmodernism truly is the high and holy religion of godless secular humanism. Thanks mostly to the French (think Rabelais, Voltaire, and Rousseau), humanism became the predominant anti-Christian worldview of the late 17th, 18th, 19th, and

20th centuries. Secular humanists replaced God with human reason and, for a while, it appeared to be working.

Thanks to the advent of modernism and the industrial revolution, quality of life improved for Western civilization. Mankind saw advances in art, music, medicine, government, modern conveniences, transportation, and a (supposed) scientific explanation of our origins. It appeared man was the master of his universe and the captain of his own salvation. And then came two numbers that rattled the very foundations of secular humanism: #1 and #2.

World Wars I and II decimated Europe. More blood was spilled in these two wars than every other human conflict in history combined. Suddenly, man didn't know everything. In fact, it appeared he knew nothing. After all, a worldview that results in that much carnage cannot be trustworthy or correct.

At the crumbling of the Berlin Wall in 1989, postmodernism became the new prevailing worldview for humanity. It was official; truth was now to be determined by each of us, individually. Whether a person's beliefs are preposterous or not, they are still true, for them. My truth is my truth, whether it is your truth or not.

Postmodernism sounds like this, "I believe in reincarnation and you believe in a resurrection; even though these two ideas completely contradict one another, neither of us is wrong. We are both right."

Trust me, I have spoken to more postmodern Christians (if there can be such a thing) than I can count. If I had to cite a statistic, I would guess that over 90 percent of Bible-belt Christian kids are partially or thoroughly postmodern. They sound like this, "Yes, I am a Christian, but hey, if you are a Buddhist, that's cool. I would never say that a non-Christian is wrong." Even children raised in conservative Christian homes have not been left unscathed by postmodernism. They sound like this, "Of course I believe homosexuality is a sin, but whatever. As long as they don't hurt anyone, what do I care?"

The obvious problem with postmodernism is that it stands in stark contradiction to Jesus' definition of truth. Jesus claimed to be the truth and the sole source and authority of truth (John 14:6). In one sentence, Jesus definitively put the nail into the postmodern coffin. We need to do the same.

> I am the way, and *the truth*, and the life; no one comes to
> the Father but through Me" (John 14:6; emphasis added).

What worldview would Jesus be? Not postmodern.

Refuting Postmodernism

There are two ways to refute this pernicious worldview; the first means is somewhat beneficial, but the second way is definitive. You can quickly show the absurdity and lack of consistency in the postmodern mindset with statements like this:

> ➤ Postmoderns definitively claim that nobody can definitively know the truth. That is a self-refuting statement.
> ➤ Postmoderns claim there is no definitive truth. Does that include that statement?
> ➤ Postmoderns do not live their worldview. When the clerk requests $14.82, a postmodern doesn't hand them a Lincoln and say, "I believe the price is only five dollars."
> ➤ Postmoderns claim to be moral, but morality cannot exist if there is not an objective moral standard. Without God, morality is only a preference, but it can never be objectively moral for all times and in every situation. The postmodern may not prefer rape and murder, but he/she can never say those acts are objectively immoral.

Use reason and logic to show the fallacies of postmodernism, but remember, their ability to logic and reason through spiritual issues is completely broken.

> But a natural man *does not accept* the things of the Spirit of God, for they are foolishness to him; and he *cannot understand them*, because they are spiritually appraised (1 Corinthians 2:14; emphasis added).

Besides, if you can argue a person into a worldview, someone can argue them out of it. Reason and logic is on the side of Christianity, but clever atheists can unwind the reason you try to persuade them to believe. It is best to use reason and logic sparingly to support your argument, but not to win the argument.

A Better Way

There is a more powerful, supernatural tool the Christian should use to dismantle postmodernism: the Bible. Why use mere words when you have a two-edged sword? Use the Bible to demolish postmodernism. It can sound something like this:

➤ Postmodernism is wrong because God says it's wrong.
➤ Postmodernism is antithetical to the Word of God; therefore, it is wrong.
➤ Postmodernism is condemned in the Bible. A postmodern man is a man who is double-minded and unstable in all his ways (James 1: 5–8).
➤ Postmodernism claims there is no truth; Jesus claims He is the truth. We trust Jesus because He rose from the dead.

Reason and logic sit at the feet of the Bible. Use Scripture as your primary weapon to refute false religions and aberrant worldviews. Might I suggest you go so far as to give an ultimatum to your children?

Make it clear to your children that postmodernism and Christianity are incompatible and cannot coexist:

> Son/daughter, if you choose the side of postmodernism, then you are at odds with Jesus Christ, who claimed to be the truth. Don't deceive yourself and be a double-minded man/woman. Surrender totally to God's Word and His authority, or you can look forward to hearing, "Depart from me you worker of iniquity, I never knew you."

Yes, this is that urgent and serious. The world-system wants your child, and the devil has had plenty of experience and success in accomplishing that goal. Set up battle lines and defend them at all costs with God's only ordained weapon, the Word.

– Reset –

If your children have only been taught Bible stories as morality tales, it is time to correct their thinking and teach the Bible as historical fact.

Chapter 18

Don't Cling Too Tightly or Hold Too Loosely

Have you ever seen a child's face fall because you humiliated them? I have. I crushed my daughter.

My eldest was 17 when our family visited the home of a friend for dinner. As we stood in the foyer with their adult children, my friend said, "We have a huge big screen downstairs. If the young people want to watch a movie and not have to listen to old people talk, they are welcome to it."

My immediate response was a protective, "What kind of movies?"

I will never forget watching my beautiful daughter's countenance fall as she dropped her head in resignation and embarrassment. While trying to be a protective father, my daughter heard, "I decide what my children watch because they are just that, children." What's worse, I said that in front of three college-age kids.

It was in that moment I realized, uh oh, I am not doing this right. I was not transitioning. My children were becoming adults, but I saw them as toddlers who needed my constant protection and correction. You don't want to make this mistake.

Tricky

This is a tricky subject to tackle because this is the only chapter that comes dangerously close to telling you how to raise your children. The other chapters have encouraged you to doggedly focus on the salvation of your children, but this chapter tiptoes into the land of, "This is how you are supposed to parent."

Because of that, permit me to speak in generalities and let you apply the specifics if you think these ideas have any merit. These waters are very choppy and I will paddle lightly and briefly. Kindly apply the following as you see fit. If you don't like it, you can thank my second daughter, who said, "You have to keep that chapter, Dad. It's really important." So here you go.

Over-protective Parents

Parents who try to protect their children have typically been called helicopter parents. Recently, pundits have relabeled these folks "lawnmower parents." Not only do we hover over our kids, we get in front of them and mow down every obstacle so they can live a stress-free life.

If you are hovering or mowing, you may have to make the changes I failed to make at the right time. This ain't easy.

When a child goes from youth to young adult, both parent and child must make some adjustments. They want to be treated like adults, but they aren't quite there yet. They don't want to submit like a child, but you still want to have the final word. That dance has led to countless toes getting stepped on.

This is often the source of the turbulent teen years that everyone jokes about. You do not want to live through long, contentious teenage years. To minimize conflict, both parties must give a little.

➢ Children on the verge of adulthood must continue to honor and submit to Mom and Dad.
➢ Mom and Dad need to loosen the reigns and be willing to let their children goof up.

No doubt, you agree that your kids should honor and submit to you, but how do you feel about loosening the reigns? If that makes you nervous, I understand; but if you refuse to let them make bad decisions, you will not be preparing them for adulthood.

This is not to suggest that you let your child make a tragic error in judgment. You should not let your teenager go to the kegger. But we do need to be willing to let our children try out their morality wings by making decisions we disagree with.

When I treated my daughter like a child, my mistake was to not allow her to potentially make some bad decisions for herself. Trust me, you don't want to do that. It is better to let them get some egg on their face while they are home so you can help them clean it off and grow in Christian maturity.

If your child is transitioning from childhood to adulthood, may I go out on a limb and suggest you allow your children to make some bad decisions?

➤ Dad, can I buy this overpriced cell phone? Answer: Maybe.
➤ Mom, can I buy this overpriced Justin Bieber t-shirt? Answer: If you think that is a wise purchase.
➤ Dad, can I go to an R-rated movie with my friends? Answer: If you think that honors the Lord, have fun.
➤ Mom, can I have my own bank account so you don't have access to my balance? Answer: Maybe.
➤ Dad, can I stay up late even though I have to be up for school in the morning? Answer: If you think that is wise.
➤ Mom, can I go to the game instead of studying for my final? Answer: That is up to you.

I confess, there are two problems with these scenarios:

1. Each of those children should have asked, "May I," not, "Can I?"
2. Circumstances might lead you to arrive at different conclusions.

There is no formula to help you navigate through these unpredictable torrents. My point is simply to encourage you to consider giving your teenager a little leash. There are four benefits to this:

1. There are life lessons that some children only learn by making bad decisions that come with painful consequences.
2. You will be letting your child road test the values you have tried to instill.
3. You will be able to help them pick up the pieces when they crash, and instill wisdom.
4. You will help them transition into adulthood.
5. You will be letting your children do what God let's you do: make sinful decisions.

I could actually hear your tires screeching when you read number five. Let's reason together. Is it not true that your Savior gives you room to sin? He certainly does. God doesn't like it when we sin, but God let's His servants make sinful choices. God let's us do that; why shouldn't we let our kids?

Here are the benefits of letting your child actually sin.

➤ They may understand the gospel for the first time.
➤ They will be treated by you the same way God treats you.
➤ They might feel their need for a Savior after they have sinned.
➤ They might just see that Mom and Dad aren't so dumb after all.

Isn't it better to let them test their wings while they are still in the nest and you can teach them how to fly? Would you rather work through your children's sins, or let his frat buddies help him?

➤ No, you should not let them do something dangerous.
➤ No, you should not let them go to places where it is downright foolish.
➤ No, you should not let your children commit gross sins that bring a lifetime of regrets.

But may I suggest you use your wisdom and allow them to take a tumble on occasion?

Just an Idea

Here are some thoughts you can noodle around and apply as you see fit. Your mileage may vary.

➤ Do a formal sit-down meeting with your "entering puberty" child. Take them to dinner and tell them you have something very important to discuss with them. They will be dying to know.

Reassure them of your love, and compliment them for the growth you have seen in their lives. Explain that they are entering an exciting new phase of life: adulthood. Let them know you realize this is going to require both parties to make some adjustments.

While under your roof, their responsibility is to honor and obey. They may respectfully question your decisions, but ultimately, they are the ones who must submit.

Don't forget to tell them about your side of the deal. After reminding them of your great love for them and desire to help them become great

God-glorifiers, tell them you now expect more from them. But also promise them that you are going to grant them more leeway. You will no longer try to micro-manage their lives.

The more responsibility they demonstrate, the more freedom they will receive. This is not a one-time meeting; this should happen regularly as you navigate the puberty rapids. You will need to adjust as you go.

➤ Prepare for your teenagers to be a bit surly. As sweet as your little dumpling is right now, there has only been one teenager who escaped a serious case of the know-it-alls. When your little angels fail to submit, or disrespect or disobey, don't freak out or get angry. Sit down with them, talk to them like they are adults, and remind them of your meeting. Explain how they are not fulfilling their end of the deal. Pray and get back to life.

➤ Do not be shocked when you discover they listen to really rotten music, watch bad TV shows, or go to R-rated movies. If you choose every single piece of entertainment for them, you are overprotecting your teenager and not helping him/her reach adulthood as soon as possible. I didn't say you shouldn't address their choices, but your goal is no longer to demand they act like you. Your goal is to help them make decisions that honor the Lord. If you choose to discuss their sinful decision with them, treat them like adults who made a bad decision, not as naughty children.

➤ Write two lists for each child. Make a list of all the fruit you observe. Make another list of the areas that need some growth. Share both lists regularly, in that order! Encourage more than you admonish. Try this formula; for every critique you offer, you should give five encouragements.

➤ Let the world teach them some lessons. Progressively stop lawn mowing for them. There are two ways to learn — from experience or from experienced people. If they won't listen to wisdom, then let them get educated at the school of hard knocks. There are many opportunities to do this. Let them overschedule and get a bad grade. Let them spend their money on something foolish and then lament their impetuousness.

Let them oversleep and be late for work. Then zip it. Never offer an "I told you so," just let the natural consequences do their pruning work. Don't forget, your Heavenly Father gives you enough rope to make good and bad decisions; we need to progressively do the same for our children.

➢ At the age of 18, expect them to pay increasing shares of their expenses: auto, insurance, entertainment, maybe rent. Let them start assuming adult responsibilities and let them struggle. After all, life is a struggle.

Those are my suggestions you can take or leave. But here is the counsel of the wisest man in the world that you would do well to follow: do not intimidate or yell at your children unless they are crossing the street without looking.

Solomon did not shout at his sons, he pleaded with them to receive his wisdom. Solomon did not bark, he implored. You can feel His fatherly heart in the Proverbs as he begs his sons to be wise. Listen to him entreat his teenagers.

> Hear, my son, your father's instruction and do not forsake your mother's teaching (Proverbs 1:8).

> My son, if you will receive my words and treasure my commandments within you, make your ear attentive to wisdom, incline your heart to understanding (Proverbs 2:1–2).

> My son, do not forget my teaching, but let your heart keep my commandments (Proverbs 3:1).

> Hear, O sons, the instruction of a father, and give attention that you may gain understanding, for I give you sound teaching; do not abandon my instruction (Proverbs 4:1–2).

> Hear, my son, and accept my sayings and the years of your life will be many (Proverbs 4:10).

> My son, give attention to my words; incline your ear to my sayings (Proverbs 4:20).

> My son, give attention to my wisdom, incline your ear to my understanding (Proverb 5:1).

> Now then, my sons, listen to me and do not depart from
> the words of my mouth (Proverbs 5:7).

Solomon did not over-protect his children by locking them up; he pleaded with them to be wise. We would do well to follow his example.

Under-protective Parents

The other side of the protective parenting coin is the parent who is a bit deistic. They give birth to their kids, but pretty much let nature take its course after that.

The under-protective parent does not guard the hearts and minds of their children. They allow their children to be exposed to images, words, and experiences that children should not experience.

The fundamental difference between childhood and adulthood is *knowledge*. What keeps a kid a kid is not necessarily his/her maturity; it is their knowledge of the world. Hence the phrase, "the innocence of children."

If you do not shield your young'uns from adult knowledge, then you will be burdening them with knowledge they should not possess. You will be forcing a child to be an adult when they are simply not ready.

Failure to protect your children will exhaust and anger them. They need you and want you to protect them and run your household. A child is too young to run a home; that is your job.

Shield your young children from bad films, TV shows, music, friends, teachers, neighbors, and Internet dangers. Anything that desires to teach your children adult things must be blocked at all costs.

Unfortunately today, our kids get exposed to far too much sexual information from sordid sources. Therefore, we need to talk to our kids about the birds and the bees far earlier than we would like. Just be age appropriate; a 4-year-old doesn't need to know as much as a 14-year-old.

Let your child fall down. Let them play. Let them get their clothes dirty. But whatever you do, guard their tender hearts. You are the gatekeeper to your young child's mind. Protect it tenaciously.

Tension

Do you feel the tension? We need to protect our young'uns, and let our teenagers make adult decisions that may be sinful. At what age should you make that transition? It depends on the child. Transitioning is not an event; it's a process that demands wisdom. The physical demands of parenting a toddler pale in comparison to the mental energy required to wisely parent a teen.

Finding the right balance with each child requires great wisdom, patience, prayer, and courage. But find it you must, or you will damage your child.

➤ If you protect too much, they will resent you.
➤ If you protect too little, they will get hurt, and resent you.
➤ If you protect too much, they will not learn lessons only experience can teach.
➤ If you protect too little, they will think you are apathetic and don't love them.

May I encourage you to sit down with your spouse and ask each other some questions?

➤ Do you think we are protecting our kids enough?
➤ Do you think we are protecting our kids too much?
➤ Are we burdening our little kids with too much information?
➤ Do we need to start letting our teenager make some bad choices?
➤ Do you think we need to have that "transition talk" with any of our kids?

Be wise like Solomon; don't chide, instead beg your teenagers to listen to your hard-won wisdom. Don't grow discouraged or frustrated; finding the correct balance requires more equilibrium than a ballerina.

You are going to make mistakes. Your kids are going to make mistakes. Don't get frustrated; dip into the gospel, forgive, forget, and press on.

On behalf of my second daughter, thank you for considering this.

– Reset –

If you are over- or under-protecting your children, you are not teaching them to love Jesus, you are teaching them to resent you.

Chapter 19

Take Yourselves Off the Hook, Mom and Dad

Yeah, I know how you feel: you have blown it a million times. You are not the only parent who makes a hash of parenting. May I remind you that you can feel remorse over your failures, but you cannot feel guilty about your failures?

Yes, you and I have sinned against our kids countless times. You now have a decision to make: what are you going to do with this potentially new-found knowledge? Feeling guilty is not an option.

Remorse over failures is natural and not sinful. Feeling guilty is sinful, because you are not guilty anymore. If you are in Christ, the guilt of the sins you have committed against your children has been erased by Jesus (Ephesians 1:7). It is time to rest in that truth. The next time your conscience misfires and screams, "Guilty," respond with the truth that Jesus has declared you not guilty.

Don't let your sins drag you into depression. Instead, may I implore you to consider doing something far more radical, and potentially life altering?

➤ Make a list of all of the sins you can remember committing against your children. You, like me, need a fair amount of time and paper to do this.
➤ Tell God you are sorry for being a bad representative to His children.
➤ Thank Him for sending His Son to receive the punishment we deserve for sinning against God and His little ones.

171

Let that sink into your head until it affects your heart. Then let the joy of the Lord be your strength. Let the knowledge that Jesus died for you, a very, very, very bad parent, serve as the motivation to turn your knowledge into action.

Let your sins drive you to the foot of the Cross. Stay there until you know that your sins are covered in the blood that flows from that tree. Let the gospel motivate you to strive harder and alter your course where necessary.

Then, gather the kiddos and confess your sins to them too. Now that is radical Christianity.

Backsliders Don't Exist

Perhaps you are grieving because you fear you have raised a "backslider." Then I have some good news for you: there is no such thing as a Christian backslider.

This may come as a shock to you, but if a child backslides, it indicates he/she never slid forward in the first place. That child is a false convert. Jesus was repeatedly blunt about this: those who put their hand to the plow and then turn back are not fit for the kingdom of God (Luke 9:62).

Here are a few more verses from Jesus that plainly teach there is a difference between a mere professor of the faith and a genuine possessor of the faith.

> Jesus said, "Then they will deliver you to tribulation, and will kill you, and you will be hated by all nations because of My name. At that time *many will fall away* and will betray one another and hate one another" (Matthew 24:9–10; emphasis added).

> Jesus said, "*Not everyone* who says to Me, 'Lord, Lord,' will enter the kingdom of heaven, but he who does the will of My Father who is in heaven will enter" (Matthew 7:21; emphasis added).

> Jesus said, "This people honors Me with their lips, But their heart is *far away from Me*" (Matthew 15:8; emphasis added).

> Jesus said, "In a similar way these are the ones on whom seed was sown on the rocky places, who, when they hear the word, immediately receive it with joy; and they have no firm

root in themselves, but are only temporary; then, when affliction or persecution arises because of the word, immediately *they fall away* And others are the ones on whom seed was sown among the thorns; these are the ones who have heard the word, but the worries of the world, and the deceitfulness of riches, and the desires for other things enter in and *choke the word*, and it becomes unfruitful. And those are the ones on whom seed was sown on the good soil; and they hear the word and accept it and bear fruit, thirty, sixty, and a hundredfold" (Mark 4:16–20; emphasis added).

Jesus described true and false converts as wheat and tares (Matthew 13:24–30), wise virgins and foolish virgins (Matthew 25:1–12), good fish and rotten fish (Matthew 13:47–50).

Needless to say, Jesus was crystal clear: there are people who claim to be in the faith, but aren't.

- ➤ If your child leaves home and loses his faith, it demonstrates he never had a saving faith to begin with (1 John 2:19).
- ➤ If God began a good work in your child, He will finish it (Philippians 1:6).
- ➤ Because nobody can get snatched from the saving hand of Jesus, if your child appears to be snatched, it is proof that your child was never in His hand to begin with (John 10:28).
- ➤ If your child examines himself and sees that he is not in the truth, it's because he isn't (2 Corinthians 13:5).

There are many more verses that discuss true and false conversions (2 Peter 2:20–22; James 2:14; 1 John 1:6–8; 2 Timothy 4:3–4), but I think you get the point. False converts can sort of act like true converts, but true converts cannot become false converts.

If you define a backslider as "a genuine Christian who stumbles and "falls into sin," fine. But the Bible does not give us permission to define a backslider as someone who names the name of Christ and then dives into an ongoing lifestyle of sin. According to the Apostle John, that person is not a Christian; he/she is a child of the devil (1 John 3:8–9).

Knowing that children who don't act like Christians aren't Christians is actually good news.

1. It is much better to come to the chilling reality that you may not be living with a genuine convert before he/she leaves home and you lose influence.
2. You can now give laser-like focus on your child's salvation.

Wouldn't you rather identify the status of your child's soul while he/she is under your roof? At least you can do something about it. You can now work with God on the regeneration of your child's heart. After all, that is precisely what God wants to do — save your children.

God's Preference

God has written millions of prodigal stories with very happy endings. Your children are not beyond God's ability to save. We serve a kind, gracious, redeeming God who loves to rescue prodigals.

Yes, God will send millions, potentially billions of people to hell, but that is not His preference. God prefers to save people, including your children. Puritan Thomas Watson said,

> God is *more inclined* to mercy than wrath. Mercy is His darling attribute, which He *most delights in* (Micah 7:18).
>
> Mercy pleases Him. Acts of severity are rather forced from God: He does not afflict willingly (Lamentations 3:33). The bee naturally gives honey, it stings only when provoked. Just so, God does not punish till He can bear no longer [Jeremiah 44:22].
>
> Mercy is God's right hand that He is most used to; inflicting punishment is called His strange work [Isaiah 38:21] (emphasis added).[1]

Scripture is clear, God is a saving God who prefers to save rather than condemn.

> This is good and acceptable in the sight of God our Savior, who *desires all men to be saved* and to come to the knowledge of the truth (1 Timothy 2:3–4; emphasis added).

> Do I take *any pleasure* in the death of the wicked? declares the Sovereign LORD. Rather, am I not *pleased* when they turn from their ways and live (Ezekiel 18:23; NIV; emphasis added)?

---

1. Thomas Watson, "The Mercy of God," https://www.monergism.com/thethreshold/sdg/mercyofgod.html.

> For I take *no pleasure* in the death of anyone, declares the Sovereign LORD. Repent and live (Ezekiel 18:32; NIV, emphasis added)!

> The Lord is not slow in keeping his promise, as some understand slowness. Instead he is patient with you, *not wanting anyone to perish*, but everyone to come to repentance (2 Peter 3:9; NIV; emphasis added).

It is never too late for a child to be born again, even if he/she no longer lives in your zip code. The seeds you have planted may sprout in surprising ways. Do not lose hope. God's timing is often much different than ours.

Do Not Feel Guilty

You should not feel guilty about the state of your child's soul. That's right — you are not responsible for your child's salvation any more than you are responsible for their glorification. If your child is not showing signs of regeneration, take yourself off the hook that God doesn't have you on.

You and I cannot save our children and we cannot make them backslide. Feel free to take a moment and breathe a deep sigh of relief. You and I can be the best parents in the world, and yet our kids could grow up to be mega-blasphemers.

Solomon's son, Jeroboam, turned out to be a wholehearted pagan idolater (1 Kings 12:31–33). The smartest man in the world raised a son who was a complete disaster. Why? Because nobody can get anybody saved. Not Solomon, not David (who had a prodigal named Absalom), and not you.

Aaron's children grew up in and around the temple. Certainly his kids would all get saved. Au contraire. Two of his kids, Nadab and Abihu, offered "strange fire" instead of rightly worshiping the Lord (Leviticus 10:1–2). Don't forget, Aaron was a high priest whose kids saw more religion than most children, and they were slain by God for their idolatry.

In the Book of Ruth, we see two widowers who lived with their Jewish mother-in-law, Naomi. Ruth got saved; Orpah did not (Ruth 1:14). Did Naomi do something that would cause one daughter-in-law to worship the true God of Israel, and the other to return to the pagan worship of Chemosh? Nope.

Parents can raise three God-fearing children, but the next three can turn out to be Tasmanian Devils. These parents raised all of them the same way, but they did not cause the first three to get saved and they can't cause the second three to be lost.

You and I are not our children's Holy Spirit. You and I can do absolutely nothing to cause our kids to become Christians. God must make Himself known to them (Ephesians 1:6). The Bible is quite clear, salvation is of the Lord (Jonah 2:4).

Whether you are a Calvinist or an Arminian, can we agree that humans do not save other humans? God, and God alone, saves. Agreed?

> For *by grace* you have been saved through faith; and that not of yourselves, it is the *gift of God*; not as a result of works, so that no one may boast (Ephesians 2:8–9).

> . . . with gentleness correcting those who are in opposition, if perhaps God may *grant them repentance* leading to the knowledge of the truth (2 Timothy 2:25; emphasis added).

If you currently have a prodigal, would you please embrace the fact that you did not cause your child to wander? If you are currently raising a child, would you please embrace the fact that you cannot do anything to save him/her?

You and I cannot determine the eternal destiny of our children. And we most certainly cannot cause them to lose their faith (as if such a thing were possible). You can't get 'em saved and you can't get 'em lost.

Nothing and Everything

So what is the point of parenting if we can't get our kids saved? While it is true that you can do nothing to get your child saved, you can do everything to be faithful to raise your children in the discipline and admonition of the Lord. That's it; your assignment is faithfulness, not conversion.

You are not responsible for the state of your child's soul; but you are responsible to love, model, nurture, instruct, and disciple your child. You can either work with or against God in accomplishing that task.

There is nothing you can do to save your child, but there is everything you can do to make sure that you faithfully lead your child to the Lord. You can either be an obedient, God-glorifying parent, or you can continue sinning. But you don't get to play the role of Savior; that job is taken.

Your job is to live, teach, and model the Gospel of Jesus Christ to your children, not make them have faith in Jesus Christ. Your parental job description is that simple and yet that complex. Knowing that salvation is of the Lord, there are some things we should keep in mind as we pray for our child's conversion.

Be Slow to Baptize and Give Assurance

As a rule, you should not baptize your children at an early age. There are two things that you should consider before you dunk a child:

1. Do they exhibit UNIQUE fruit that they never exhibited before? Don't look for the fruit that already existed before they made a profession of faith; look for fruit you have never seen before. What does that look like?

   ➤ If your child used to be selfish but now shares, that is a good sign.

   ➤ If your child never sang in church, but now he/she warbles away, that is new fruit.

   ➤ If your little nightmare suddenly becomes compliant and sweet, then you are seeing new fruit.

2. You might want to wait to baptize your child until puberty hits. This is not a perfect rule, but there is a reason that most societies make adolescence the time of passage from childhood to adulthood. Confirmations, first communions, bar and bat mitzvahs all take place at puberty time. You should consider your child's awareness of their sexual feelings so they fully understand what it Jesus means when He says, "If anyone wishes to come after Me, he must deny himself, and take up his cross and follow Me" (Matthew 16:24).

Too many kids get baptized at a young age, only to later realize they really had not repented and trusted Jesus. You don't want to cause this confusion.

Be careful to neither affirm nor deny your child's salvation. Don't squash their tender hearts, but don't give assurance to their little hearts either. Little children are going to sing "Jesus loves me" because kids typically do what Mom and Dad do. Affirm their love for Jesus, but do not give your young child assurance of salvation. That is not your job; assurance is the exclusive work of the Holy Spirit (Romans 8:16).

Don't Delay

May I encourage you to apply what you have learned now? As in, today. Do not wait until you have improved your Christian parenting skills to repent before your children. Call them together stat.

Repent toward your children before the sun goes down. Ask them to forgive you. Tell them what you have learned and promise them you are going to try and be a different Mommy or Daddy. Ask them for a fresh start. It's never too late.

But you protest, "I really, really blew it with my kids." Perhaps you did; then confess your sins to the Lord and to your children, and know that you are really, really forgiven (1 John 1:8). Let this wonderful knowledge be the very thing that fuels your desire to live out your faith for your children.

Know that you are going to fail again and again. You are going to forget this teaching regularly. Be grateful for so great a salvation and then get back to discipling your children.

What should you do to remind yourself to be a parent who is influenced and affected by the gospel? Remember that you are the chief sinner in your house who has been completely and totally forgiven. Continue in His Word. Never stop reading your Bible. Utilize the means of grace as if your life and the life of your family, depends on it. Because it does.

When you forget and sin, repent and get back in the saddle and keep moving forward. Strive to be a faithful parent and leave the results to the God who loves your child more than you do.

– Reset –

Do you need to let your self off the hook for your child's salvation and trust the Lord who loves your children more than you do?

Chapter 20

Questions for Parents

The following is a list of all of the questions I have asked you throughout this book. They are compiled here for your convenience.

- ➢ Use this to test yourself to see how you have been doing as a parent, and reorient yourself if necessary.
- ➢ Use this to see how many times you have failed.
- ➢ Use this to remember how many times you have been forgiven by God.
- ➢ Use this regularly to remind yourself of your Christian duties to your children.

Before you dive into this, don't forget — you are NOT the world's first perfect parent. You will see many, many shortcomings. Remember, your sins were nailed to a tree two thousand years ago (Colossians 2:14). Let this list reorient you if necessary, but do not let this list make you feel guilty, because you are not guilty anymore. Use this list to lead you to joy, not despair.

Chapter 1: Stop Disciplining and Start Discipling

Have you been disciplining without discipling?

Are you persuaded that you need to make an adjustment?

Do you remember the simple sentence parents should remember before engaging their child?

How does God respond to you when you sin?

Do you need to repent to your children for how you have sinned against them?

Should you ever spank in anger?

Chapter 2: Show Them the Gospel

When you sin against your children, do you ever ask for their forgiveness?

When your children sin, do they ever hear an encouraging word from a fellow sinner?

When your children sin against each other, do you force them to "say you're sorry," or do you go to the heart of the issue: sin, forgiveness, and reconciliation?

When the temperature of your house heats up, do you ever put your faith on display by working through issues biblically?

When you run into conflict, do you argue like the chief of sinners?

When your house gets tense, are you responding in light of the gospel that says you are the worst sinner in the house?

When your spouse or children correct you, do you listen with pride, or with humility because you recognize that you are a far bigger sinner than they are?

When your spouse sins against you, do you get offended and angry because you think you deserve better? Or do you respond with the attitude that says, "I am the chief of sinners who deserves hell, so this ain't nothing!"

When your bedroom is chilly, do you respond with warmth because you do not insist on your own way?

How does God treat you when you sin? How patient has God been with you? Would you like God to treat you the way you treat your kids?

Bonus: If you happen to think pride is not an issue for you, here are just ten questions to help you see that you are just like the rest of us Pride Monsters.

You have pride if:

1. You want to be well known or well respected (Isaiah 14:13–15; James 3:13–16; Romans 12:6).

2. You like to impress people (Luke 10:38–42) or receive recognition and praise (John 5:41–44; Matthew 6:1, 23:5–7).

3. You like to talk about yourself.

4. You are deceitful about your failures or shortcomings (Psalm 24:3–4, 26:2–4; Jeremiah 48:10; Proverbs 26:20–26).

5. You have a fear of man problem that manifests itself in your desire for others to think highly of you (Proverbs 29:25).

6. You are a perfectionist who can't stand for anything to be sub-par because it reflects poorly on you.

7. You feel superior to others (Romans 12:3, 16; James 2:1–4).

8. You feel deserving and lack gratitude because you think you deserve the good things you have (Luke 17:11–19; Ephesians 5:19–20; 1 Thessalonians 5:16–18; Colossians 3:15–17; Philippians 2:14).

9. You are captive to self-pity because you are convinced you deserve better.

10. You are jealous and envious because you think you should have the stuff others own (James 3:13–16).

Chapter 3: Have Your Children Submit to the Right Authority

When you tell your child to behave a certain way, do you explain why?

Why should your child obey you?

Who is supposed to be the chief authority in your child's life — you or God? Who do they think it is?

Have you been practicing the "submit to me" approach or the "submit to God" approach?

Do your kids know that our temporal experience has a string attached to God? Do they know that earth is a reflection of heaven? Do they know that the human experience is first found in God?

Chapter 4: Instill the Fear of the Lord

Are you afraid to teach your children to fear the Lord?

Does your child fear the Lord, love the Lord, or both?

Does your child fear you? If so, what kind of fear do they have: servile or respectful fear?

Do you think your child is at a level of accountability?

Chapter 5: Make Sure They Hear the Correct Gospel

Do you preach the gospel to your children?

Do you preach the correct gospel to your children?

If asked, could your child accurately present the gospel?

Which gospel does your child believe?

Chapter 6: Make Sure You Rightly Apply the Law

Have you ever opened up the law for your child?

Has your child been made to understand the exceeding sinfulness of sin?

Have you helped them to understand that they will not be judged based on the standard of Adolph Hitler, but they will be judged based on the perfect, righteous, and holy standard of God?

Have your children ever trembled before a just and holy law?

Chapter 7: Don't Lose Your Balance

Does your child know the difference between the law and the gospel?

Which do you present more, law or gospel?

What is your child's motivation for obedience?

Is your child a Do-Do-Do Christian? If so, what are you going to tell him/her?

Is your child a Bruised Reed Christian? If so, what are you going to tell him/her?

Does your child think he/she is a Second-class Christian? If so, what are you going to tell him/her?

Does your child think that Christianity is about rule keeping, or grace that motivates rule keeping?

Chapter 8: Command Your Child to Repent and Trust

Has your child asked Jesus into his/her heart, made Jesus Lord and Savior, said the sinner's prayer, or committed to Jesus?

Has your child repented and trusted Jesus Christ?

Does your child understand repentance?

Does your child understand what it means to have faith in Jesus?

Chapter 9: Don't Confuse Justification with Sanctification

Does your child know the difference between justification and sanctification?

Are you preaching justification and sanctification in equal measures?

Chapter 10: Prepare Your Child to Meet Other Suitors

Have your children heard the lashes that Jesus received as the cat-o-nine tales shredded His back?

Have they heard the sickening thud of the punches that landed squarely on the Lord of Glory's face?

Have they felt the spit that splattered the diamond of heaven?

Do they know their God was stripped naked and mocked by the very creatures He created to be His image bearers?

Have you shown your child the tender area of the wrist where nails were driven through the hands of the Carpenter of Galilee? Have you shown your kids the tender area of the Achilles heel where nails were slammed through the feet of the One who walked on water?

Have they heard King Jesus gasping for breath until He died from suffocation?

Does your child know what was accomplished for them by Jesus? Have they been awed by the effects of the gospel?

When was the last time your family heard about the wrath of God? When was the last time you heard a sermon that made you and your children fear God?

What kind of prayers do you pray with your kids? What theology do they learn from you when you pray?

What kind of music do your kids digest? Is it robustly theological or does it focus on one theme over and over?

Do your kids see Jesus as the most spectacular entity in the universe?

Chapter 11: Teach Your Children How the Bible Works

Do your kids understand how the Bible works (how it flows)?

Do your kids understand how the Bible works (how it applies)?

Do your kids know how to read the Bible and rightly divide the truth?

Do your kids know the Bible is not a morality book?

Do your kids know how to make a decision about spouses, houses, and automobiles?

Chapter 12: Don't Torque Your Kids

Have you made any parenting mistakes that have angered your children? Do you need to repent to them for these sins?

When you discipline your child:

➢ What is your tone and volume?

➢ What does your face say?

➢ Is your discipline about correcting their behavior or addressing the state of their relationship with God?

Chapter 13: Act Like a Good Shepherd

Have you checked your kid's listening device to learn what kind of music they are into?

Do your children know that theology is important?

Does your child know the importance of correct theology and the consequences of heresy?

Do they know the early Church fought over the Greek letter i?

Chapter 14: Don't Let Them Be Degraded or Shunned at Church

Has your church been honoring your teenagers, or degrading them by pressuring them to participate in gross-out games?

Does your teenager feel welcomed and loved by the adults at your church?

Does your child feel loved, shunned, respected, or degraded at church?

Chapter 15: Answer the Big "Why" Questions

Do your children know the purpose of their existence?

Do your children obey immediately when you command them?

Do they respond cheerfully when you call them to do a chore?

Do they happily obey you because they are submitting to God?

Do your children understand that they are not their jobs?

Would you like your child to be a vessel of honor used by the Lord for lofty things or common things?

Chapter 16: Enroll Them in Ancestry.com/Protestantism

Have your children met their spiritual ancestors?

Do your children know they have a long, illustrious heritage of brave men and women who died for the faith delivered once for all time?

Chapter 17: Put Armor on Your Children

Do you read the Bible to your children as if God Himself wrote it?

Do you teach the Bible to your children like it is the infallible, inerrant, sufficient revelation of God to man? Do you teach them to honor the Word of God?

Do your children know that the Bible is not a storybook filled with tall tales of longhaired strong men and prophets who spend three-day weekends in the belly of a big fish?

Have you ever taught your children creation science?

Have you considered giving an ultimatum to your child: either trust the Bible totally or forsake it completely?

Chapter 18: Don't Cling Too Tightly or Hold Too Loosely

Do you think you are protecting your kids too much?
Do you think you are protecting them enough?
Are you burdening your little kids with too much information?
Do we need to start letting our teenager make some bad choices?
Do you think you should ever let your child sin?

Chapter 19: Take Yourselves Off the Hook, Mom and Dad

Do you know the difference between remorse and guilt?
Who do you believe can save your child, you or God?
Does your child exhibit new fruit due to regeneration?
Does your child act like a Christian or an unbeliever?
Do you believe that your child can lose his/her salvation?
Would God prefer to damn or save your child?
Who loves your child more, you or God?

Now What?

Now that you have been reminded how far short you have fallen, what should you do? That's right! Run to Jesus and then press on.

Your parenting sins are forgiven and forgotten by God. You need to forget them too. Remember His kindness to you, then train up your children in the fear and the admonition of the Lord.

Let your parenting sins remind you that you need Jesus every day. Let your parenting sins drive you to the Cross where you can beckon your family to join you.

Oh, and don't forget to not make your kids nuts.

Submit to Me vs. Submit to God Scenarios

Here are some more common parenting conversations that may help tether your child to God and His Word, not to you and your dictates.

Parental submission approach: You are going to go to the art museum with us and you are going to enjoy it whether you like it or not.

Submission to God approach: Honey, take a look at that sunset. It's gorgeous, isn't it? Do you know who painted that for you? God, the greatest artist the world has ever known. When we study beautiful art that rightly reflects an attribute of God, we are, in a sense, studying God. Let's go to the museum and learn something about our artistic God.

Parental submission approach: Just because you have a crummy voice doesn't mean you shouldn't worship in church. Now sing!

Submission to God approach: Honey, do you know why we sing? Because God sings (Zephaniah 3:17). When we sing, we are expressing our emotions the way God does. In fact, there is no loftier form of expression than singing poetry to God; that is what worship is. Oh, and don't forget, God despises heartless on-pitch singing, but He loves tone-deaf worship from the heart (John 4:24). He loves it.

Parental submission approach: Dissect those sentences or you is gonna turn out all dumm.

Submission to God approach: Honey, we are having meat-loaf for dinner. If I asked you what we are having for dinner tonight, you would know the answer because I have communicated it to you. Now, if I said, "Honey, we befuddled the watermelon sky because of the delicious Chevrolets," you wouldn't have any idea what I was trying to say.

When we study grammar, we are learning to be like our communicating God. When God speaks, He always communicates clearly and well. If we are going to be like Him, then we should strive to be the same. Now, don't forget to never end a sentence with a preposition.

Parental submission approach: You better not sneak into that concert or you will end up in the hoosegow.

Submission to God approach: Honey, do you remember when we discussed "the economic subordination of the Trinitarian godhead?"

When we submit to authorities, we are acting like the Trinity. If you don't submit to the authorities God has put in place for our good, then you have committed an even greater crime — you have disobeyed God. If you want the swift sword of justice to fall on you, break the law. If you want to reflect God, then submit to the authorities and don't sneak into that concert.

Oh, and before you run off to the show, don't forget that justice exists because God is just (Psalms 33:5; Isaiah 61:8). There are jails on earth because there is a jail for lawbreakers in eternity. Now, don't forget your earplugs.

Parental submission approach: It's time for you to find yourself a good woman and tie the knot. And she better be a believer or you can forget about getting anymore Christmas presents from us.

Submission to God approach: Honey, God has forever been about the gospel. In fact, the Bible says that God created the universe so souls could be saved and God could be glorified for being an amazing Savior (Ephesians 2:1–10). God sent His Son to die in the place of sinners and He wants the world to know about it.

Did you know that when you get married, you will have the privilege of participating with God in the saving of lost souls?

When you get married, the husband plays the role of Jesus, and the wife plays the role of the Church (Ephesians 5:32).

If the world watches you and sees how you treat one another, they will actually be seeing the gospel on display in your relationship. That is why it is so important that you choose wisely and not marry an unbeliever. If you do, you won't get to proclaim the gospel to the watching world.

Not only that — we are commanded to not become unequally yoked with an unbeliever (2 Corinthians 6:14) because it distorts the picture it is supposed to represent. Not to mention, you will both be miserable.

Parental submission approach: Of course wedding rings are expensive, but that's just the way we do it. Now go to the jewelry store or you are going to spend the rest of your life on Christian Mingle.

Submission to God approach: Honey, look at that rainbow. Do you know what it symbolizes? Correct, it is a physical sign of a promise God made to never drown the world again (Genesis 9:13).

Do you know what circumcision is in the Old Testament? It is an external mark that demonstrates you are a part of the Mosaic covenant. Covenants always have an accompanying physical seal to remind ourselves and the world that we are in a "'til death do us part" contract.

When we give our new spouse a wedding ring, we are giving them a seal of our marriage covenant. When we wear an external sign of an inward commitment to be loyal and faithful to our life-long covenant partner, we are being biblical.

By the way, a celebratory covenant meal typically took place after the covenant was cut. That is what Jesus was doing when He instituted the Lord's Supper after announcing the new covenant. That is why we take communion. That is also why we have wedding receptions — it is a celebratory meal, just like in the Bible. Oh, and don't forget, the covenant partners would also feed each other at this meal as a way of saying, "I will do anything for you." So make sure you don't smash the cake into your spouse's face; that isn't biblical.

Parental submission approach: Put this abstinence ring on, and don't you dare lose your virginity until you get married.

Submit to God approach: Take a seat, Teenager, we need to have the talk. Don't panic, this is not going to be a "how to make babies talk," this is going to be a "why sex exists talk."

You know that sex outside of marriage is a sin against God and it is a sin against your body (1 Corinthians 6:9, 18). But I want to give you a very profound reason for you to abstain from the wonderful, God ordained, pleasurable act of sex until you are married. Here goes.

There is a reason we see so much sexual confusion these days. People are groping to figure out why intimacy just doesn't satisfy. That is why they keep trying new partners and new configurations and different genders. The unregenerate man or woman will never, ever be satisfied with sex because they do not understand that the meaning of sex is transcendent.

Marital intimacy is a foretaste of the intimacy that we will experience when our heavenly bridegroom consummates His wedding with the Church (Ephesians 5:32). Of course we will not have sex with God in heaven, but we will have an intimacy with Him that the human sexual act points toward. In other words, if you think sex is amazing, wait until you experience how incredible it will be to see God face to face. When we understand that sex is a foretaste of being glorified, then we will experience sex in its fullness.

Honey, if you have sex with someone who is not your spouse, you will not be satisfied, and you tell the world that Jesus has an intimate relationship with religions that are not His bride.

That is why we wait to have sex until we are married. We don't want to make dirty what is transcendent. We don't want to make a hash of the picture that intimacy is intended to paint. We do not want to confuse the world about the gospel.

Reminder

Please do not memorize these mini-sermons. Instead, study the Bible constantly, then simply apply your knowledge to your children.

You got this, Mom and Dad. Go get 'em.

About the Author

Todd Friel is the host of *Wretched Radio*, a daily sundicated talk radio program, as well as host of *Wretched TV*. *Wretched Radio* is heard on 600 stations nationwide and *Wretched TV* is available in over 110 million households. He is also the author of *Jesus Unmasked* and *Stressed Out*. Todd is the husband of one wife and father of three adult children.

Website: www.wretchedradio.com

Twitter: www.twitter.com/Wretchedradio

Facebook: facebook.com/wretchednetwork

OPEN & GROW

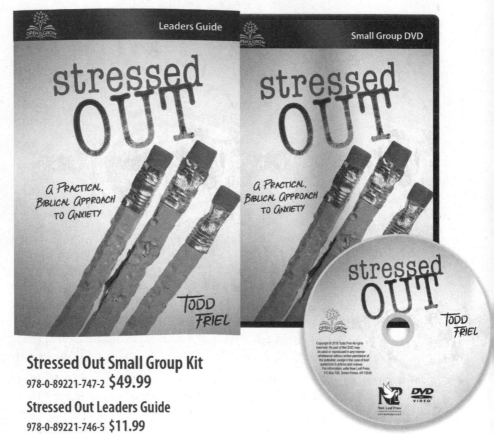

Stressed Out Small Group Kit
978-0-89221-747-2 **$49.99**

Stressed Out Leaders Guide
978-0-89221-746-5 **$11.99**

Stressed Out DVD (95 min.)
713438-10233-7 **$25.99**

Stressed Out Book
978-0-89221-743-4 **$13.99**

Includes: Leader's guide, *Stressed Out: A Practical, Biblical Approach to Anxiety* book, and DVD of practical teaching by author Todd Friel. This study is designed to be done in 5 parts lasting 60-90 minutes each and will help small groups apply Biblical truths to replace fear, anxiety, and depression with peace.

New Leaf Press
A Division of New Leaf Publishing Group
www.newleafpress.net